365
Days of
Grace

Daily devotions for
overcoming
disappointment
and offense

BroadStreet
PUBLISHING

BroadStreet Publishing Group, LLC.
Savage, Minnesota, USA
Broadstreetpublishing.com

365 Days of Grace

© 2023 by BroadStreet Publishing®

9781424565665
9781424565672 (eBook)

Devotions composed by Suzanne Niles. Statements of grace by Jeanna Harder.

Typesetting and design by Garborg Design Works | garborgdesign.com

Editorial services by Carole Holdahl

Printed in China.

23 24 25 26 27 28 29   7 6 5 4 3 2 1

A person's insight
gives him patience,
and his virtue is to
overlook an offense.

PROVERBS 19:11 CSB

Introduction

God created us for relationships; they are vital for happy, healthy living. But even the best of friends will disappoint because we are all imperfect, broken humans.

At times, the words or actions of others can leave us feeling unloved, betrayed, devalued, or rejected. God's grace is abundant in every situation and for all things. He will never let you down, and he will give you what you need to walk through the heartache of a broken relationship as well as the process of mending it.

As you meditate on these daily Scriptures, devotions, and prayers, let the Father guide you in the way you should go—leaving the offense, and loving the offender through the power of his grace. You can choose love and forgiveness because he gave those to you first. Although it might be difficult, and you likely won't get it right every time, you can rest in the knowledge that his mercies are new every morning.

Don't bury your face in your pillow; look up to God in thankfulness and praise. And always remember that you are loved, treasured, and accepted by the one who matters most.

January

"My grace is all you need. My power
works best in weakness."

2 CORINTHIANS 12:9 NLT

Trust

Trust in the LORD with all your heart
and lean not on your own understanding;
in all your ways submit to him
and he will make your paths straight.

PROVERBS 3:5-6 NIV

Friendship is a wonderful and vital connection. God created us for relationships and it's a blessing to have a confidant. Titia valued all her friends and was convinced she could trust them. Then she found out that her friend to whom she had privately revealed her secret had repeated the details as a prayer request. Titia felt betrayed and ashamed. The actions of this previously trusted person left her dealing with heartbreak and embarrassment.

There is one who never lets you down; his name is Jesus. Meditate on his Word daily and it will instruct you in the way you should go. If you need answers on how to respond to those who offend you, go to Jesus. He understands betrayal and rejection like no other. Through his Holy Spirit, he will lead you to forgiveness. He offers wisdom and discernment.

Grace upon Grace

Identify someone you can safely share your burdens with.

Yoked

Those who hope in the LORD will renew their strength.
They will soar on wings like eagles;
they will run and not grow weary,
they will walk and not be faint.

ISAIAH 40:31 NIV

If you compare the frenetic work and home life we maintain today to those a few decades ago, it makes us look like we're constantly moving at warp speed. Remember when we didn't live on our smartphones, jumping at every ring or text tone? Where did the forty-hour workweek go? We are moving at a pace that is not only zapping our strength but can leave us depleted and depressed.

There is a remedy for all who are beyond exhausted. We must take Jesus up on his offer to be yoked with him. When we're in lockstep with Christ, he carries the entire burden. There is rest and rejuvenation when we trust our Savior to shoulder the load. Knowing that he alone can supply all we need should drive us to our knees and cause us to open his Word. There we'll be revived as we sit at his feet.

Grace upon Grace

*Eliminate something from your schedule
that is sucking your time and energy.*

On Alert

Be of sober spirit, be on the alert. Your adversary, the devil, prowls around like a roaring lion, seeking someone to devour.

1 Peter 5:8 NASB

All of us have women in our lives who are not really friends. We would call them acquaintances. And sometimes there's one in particular who rubs us the wrong way. It's frustrating when she's the center of attention. Ronnie was one of those women. She was applauded no matter what she did. It seemed to Julia that she was the only one it bothered. She didn't like Ronnie even though she pretended. Then in a moment of spiritual clarity, Julia realized that she herself was deceived into thinking that she was the more deserving person.

God's Word assures us that he is the one who lifts one up and brings others low. If we humble ourselves, we silence our ego. We then have the right mindset to resist the enemy's lies which can only lead to the temptation of pride. We please the Father when we celebrate the way he uses others for his purposes. Don't ever believe Satan's deception that God has forgotten about you. Seek his will for your life, and in his timing, he will complete every perfect plan that he set for you to accomplish for his kingdom.

Grace upon Grace

Humbly ask the Lord if there is any area of pride that you need to deal with.

Shame

Uphold me according to your promise, that I may live,
and let me not be put to shame in my hope!

PSALM 119:116 ESV

Desiree was a young mom, and she had overheard a couple
of friends talking. Their conversation broke her heart and
embarrassed her. She hid her tears until she was home.
There was a big event coming up, and she was not included.
All the possible reasons they didn't want to include her
tormented her, and she was humiliated. Desiree cried for
God for those involved to correct the faux pas. The phone
didn't ring, and she sunk deeper into shame.

The Father draws you to himself, beckoning you to remain
in the shadow of his wings as he speaks. The truth is, he will
never reject you. You may miss this party, but he has given
you hope of the greatest celebration—eternity with him.
He reminds you he wanted you enough to die for you. He
whispers that you are perfection because he looks at you
and he sees his Son. You are loved, treasured, and accepted
by the one who matters most.

Grace upon Grace

*Sing a song of praise to the Father
who gives love and grace to you daily.*

Resolve

> "Naked I came from my mother's womb,
> and naked I will leave this life.
> The Lord gives, and the Lord takes away.
> Blessed be the name of the Lord."

JOB 1:21-22 CSB

Lucindy is one of those women who lives in fear that an event will occur, or a phone call will come that will alter her life. She is convinced that imminent disaster is on the horizon—a bad diagnosis, the loss of a job, or the passing of a loved one. The best approach for Lucindy is to brush off thoughts of doom and choose to live closely with the Lord. Responsibilities for daily existence, then, won't steal each moment. Instead, she can be thankful for every good blessing.

When those tragic times strike, it takes our breath away and we run the gamut of emotions. Unbelief and anger with the inexplicable loss can flood the first few moments. If we can prepare, however, knowing the best thing we can do is turn to God and praise him in the storm, we can be assured that his presence and comfort will envelop us. Regardless of what comes, we must resolve to have the faith that God will carry us through.

Grace upon Grace

*Take captive each fearful thought that enters your mind
and know that God is in control.*

Consequences

When David saw that his servants were whispering, David
perceived that the child was dead. Therefore David said to
his servants, "Is the child dead?" And they said, "He is dead."

2 SAMUEL 12:19 NKJV

There are consequences for misguided actions. If we choose
to act in a harmful way and it's a secret from others, God
still knows. When David saw Bathsheba bathing on the
rooftop, he was overcome with desire for her even though
she was not his to have. His lust led to adultery, deception,
and the murder of an innocent man. Ultimately, David's
baby boy from that union died.

Although it seemed that David's affair would be the nail in
the coffin of his moniker, "a man after God's own heart,"
it wasn't. There is forgiveness for any sin, even the most
heinous. We must accept God's discipline for our trespasses,
confess them, and be grateful for his never-ending
forgiveness. God will never reject us, but he will discipline
us so we will grow in Christ. Accept his chastening and
be thankful for a heavenly Father whose love for you is
graciously unconditional.

Grace upon Grace

Memorize a verse that offers guidance in times of temptation.

Look Up

Those who look to him are radiant;
their faces are never covered with shame.

PSALM 34:5 NIV

His mercies are new every morning! Despite what may have happened before, God is giving us another day to make better choices, restore relationships, and find new passions that will further his kingdom. There is no reason to bury our faces in a pillow, and there is every reason to look up in praise of the one who watches over us and guides our paths. We are chosen and cherished by our God!

If you hear a voice that says you aren't worthy, rebuke it immediately. When Jesus was tempted by the devil, he resisted by quoting the Word. Don't attempt to formulate your own argument, but instead imitate our Savior by saying, "It is written…." God's Word cannot be refuted, not even by Satan. It can destroy the enemy's lies when he tells you you're unloved, not good enough, or shameful. Shut Satan down with Scripture and show him you know how valuable you are to Jesus.

Grace upon Grace

*Claim the grace God freely offers
and not the shame the devil tries to throw at you.*

Righteous Road

I will exalt You, LORD, for You have lifted me up,
and have not let my enemies rejoice over me.
LORD my God, I cried to You for help,
and You healed me.

PSALM 30:1-2 NASB

When an acquaintance concocted a plan to entrap Elle,
she didn't believe it at first. The shock began to wear off,
and she tried to understand the reasons. At first, she was
just sad, and then she wondered what she ever did to this
"friend." Elle started to call another friend, Paula, because
she knew she could vent to her. It would feel so good to
gain an ally. Together they might be able to ascertain why
this acquaintance had been so conniving.

However, if Eve chooses to speak about this offense without
the right motives, she joins her perpetrator in sin. Instead
of going to Paula, she should go to Jesus. He will not only
listen intently but will also speak his ways of truth to you.
Even if the wrongdoer never repents of their scheme, God
will lift you up, heal your heart, and be very pleased that
you chose the righteous road.

Grace upon Grace

*Ask God to help you graciously forgive
and love someone who has hurt you.*

Careless

Search me, O God, and know my heart!
Try me and know my thoughts!
And see if there be any grievous way in me,
and lead me in the way everlasting!

PSALM 139:23-24 ESV

Darci woke up in the middle of the night with a nagging feeling that something was not quite right. She discounted it and tried to resume her sleep, only she couldn't. Her mind kept reeling. She rolled out of bed and found a quiet place to pray. Darci asked the Lord to search her heart, and she suddenly had a fresh perspective on her day. What was that thing she had casually said to the new woman at church? Was that what woke her up at night, giving her the restless feeling?

Sometimes we don't pay much attention to the words we use or our delivery, leaving us on the brink of breaking someone's heart. When we eventually realize how careless our conversation was, we shudder. Thankfully, we have a mercy seat where we can repent. If we want to love others for Jesus, we must think before we speak.

Grace upon Grace

*Speak words of love and encouragement
to someone the Lord puts on your heart.*

All Alone

Why do You stand far away, Lord?
Why do You hide Yourself in times of trouble?

PSALM 10:1 NASB

There is a loneliness that can envelope us, making us feel like the last person on earth. Sometimes it is because of an unfortunate event in our lives, but at other times it can be self-imposed. We cry out, begging God for some comfort. We beg him to bring us someone who cares. We cry tears of anguish yet feel numb at the same time.

If we would only recall that Jesus is a friend who sticks closer than a brother. His presence consoles us. If we actually believe that we are chosen and loved with an everlasting love, we can trust God in the times when he is silent. It is often in those quiet seasons that he makes a way for us. In his own timing he will supply all we need. In the meantime, we can trust that the very Savior who never lets us out of his sight is close by working on our behalf.

Grace upon Grace

*Spend some quiet time with the one
who will never leave you or forsake you.*

Helpers

Hear my cry, O God, listen to my prayer;
from the end of the earth I call to you
when my heart is faint.
Lead me to the rock that is higher than I,
for you have been my refuge,
a strong tower against the enemy.

PSALM 61:1-3 ESV

Ginger knocked on her fellow parishioner's door, bringing her life's problems with her. As she bombarded Francis with her issues, Francis begged God for an excuse to shorten the visit so she could get on with her own agenda. Then the voice in Fran's head reminded her of how the pastor recently preached on how we are to consider others as more important than ourselves. We are to listen and care, even if that derails our plans for the day.

We have a God who makes himself available day and night. As Christ followers, we are to imitate our Lord. When we put our lives on hold to bear the burden of others, we fulfill one of the very purposes for which God placed us on this earth. We look like Jesus when we love unselfishly, humbling ourselves to help those who belong to him.

Grace upon Grace

*Call a friend who has been wanting to connect
and prioritize time with them.*

Stand Out

> "My grace is sufficient for you,
> for my power is perfected in weakness."
>
> 2 CORINTHIANS 12:9 CSB

Polly overheard all the elaborate plans for the teen party.
Every popular kid would be there, and it would be an
absolute blast. She knew where and when it was going to be,
but she would never get the chance to see go. By standing
up for her beliefs, the other kids considered Polly weird.
She would never make the invitation list. She knew though
that she could rejoice in her suffering because her identity
was in Christ, and it was only him she wanted to please.

Rejection is one of the worst heartaches. Knowing who you
are in Christ creates a desire to stand out instead of fitting
in. Paul said that if he were trying to please men he would
not be a servant of God. Wouldn't you rather be considered
less by the world because you belong to Christ? Find your
strength in owning the position of being a child of the King.

Grace upon Grace

*Rely on God's strength to stand out as a child of the King
instead of conforming to the world.*

Always Trustworthy

Trust in Him at all times, you people;
Pour out your hearts before Him;
God is a refuge for us.

PSALM 62:8 NASB

There was a sensitive issue with which Rena was struggling. She had a hard time deciding who to talk to about it. If she shared, she would have to trust that her issue would be held in the strictest confidence. She needed counsel from someone wise and compassionate. Choosing the wrong person could lead to gossip. But entrusting herself to the right person could mean she could reach some peace in her problem.

Jesus is the one we can always trust. When we can hardly say the words through the sobs, he understands what we have endured and how it has broken us. He wants us to bring every burden to him, regardless of how heavy or ugly it may be. He draws us closely to him as he mends our fractured heart. He speaks truth into the situation and kindly reveals whether we have anything to confess or we must forgive another. He hides us under his wing and whispers his love and guidance.

Grace upon Grace

Run to the one you can always trust and be comforted.

Developing

We can rejoice, too, when we run into problems and trials,
for we know that they help us develop endurance. And
endurance develops strength of character, and character
strengthens our confident hope of salvation.

ROMANS 5:3-4 NLT

Everyone moved closer as the baby began to pull herself
up on a chair. With every unsteady movement those
closest were ready to protect her, yet they wanted to give
her the opportunity to succeed on her own. The family
smiled as the little knees worked to keep her on her feet.
Then the baby fell with a little whimper. Discouraged but
determined, the child tried again and again, and with each
encouraging accomplishment her confidence was building,
and each little gain brought growth.

God wants us to remember that we can either gain strength
and perseverance from adversity or allow it to cause us to
fall apart under the burden. If we lose hope and continually
ask, "Why?" instead of trusting in his ways, we can become
resistant to his work. Seek him in prayer and read his Word.
There, you'll find courage as the Holy Spirit opens your eyes
to see the eternal good of life lived within his purposes.

Grace upon Grace

*Go on a walk and consider God's wise
and perfect intentions for you.*

Affliction

Our momentary light affliction is producing for us an
absolutely incomparable eternal weight of glory.

2 CORINTHIANS 4:17 CSB

Regardless of the stage of life you are in, you have probably
endured some type of injury. Suddenly, that cast you are
wearing or the deep rest you need has impacted your daily
freedom. It's frustrating to need help with small tasks which
always came so naturally. It feels as though it will never
end, and you wonder if you will go back to full normality
without all these adjustments and pain. You wish you could
blink and fast track the time it will take to move on with
your life.

God desires for us have an abundant life, but he also said
in his Word that suffering will happen. That's a hard pill to
swallow, and many people reject faith in God because he
doesn't fix everything. We must remember that his ways are
high above ours. He knows the glorious outcome when we
submit to his way of working for good in us. Life is short;
eternity is forever. Run the race with patience and trust
God since before you know it, you will receive the reward.

Grace upon Grace

Soak in a renewed mindset regarding affliction and suffering.

Don't Give Up

Consider it pure joy, my brothers and sisters, whenever you face trials of many kinds, because you know that the testing of your faith produces perseverance. Let perseverance finish its work so that you may be mature and complete, not lacking anything.

JAMES 1:2-4 NIV

It was a season in which one problem followed another. There was no rest in between the barrage of burdens and Delaney was physically and mentally spent. She begged God for relief and when nothing came, she started to figure her own way out. When that didn't work well either, Delaney reverted to being on her knees and petitioning again. This time, however, she listened. She started to trust, and then rejoice. Truth flooded her mind with words like, "My grace is sufficient."

Jesus is our example. We can learn from him that intense suffering brings miraculous outcomes. We are to count it all joy when trials assail us because in time, we will emerge in the image of his Son. Don't give up. He is working something more beautiful in you than you could ever imagine.

Grace upon Grace

Repeat these words out loud, "My grace is sufficient"
as you persevere through hardship.

Heavenly Home

"There is more than enough room in my Father's home. If this were not so, would I have told you that I am going to prepare a place for you? When everything is ready, I will come and get you, so that you will always be with me where I am."

JOHN 14:2-3 NLT

Kim's anticipation was high for the upcoming trip. There was a beautiful rental house right on the beach waiting for her. She envisioned herself in a lounge chair soaking up the rays and sipping a cold drink. The phone rang and unfortunately, the house was suddenly unavailable due to an unexpected event. Kim got her money back, but her dreams of that wonderful vacation were dashed.

When we plan excitedly for something only to have it fall through, we experience great disappointment. As we trust God for the promises in his Word, we'll never encounter such a setback because he's always faithful. The place reserved for us in heaven is guaranteed. The length of time we will be there is set for eternity. Jesus said so. The accommodations will be perfectly suited to us since our Savior prepared them. If you are in Christ, you have absolute assurance that he will come to take you home.

Grace upon Grace

Write "the best is yet to come" on a sticky note somewhere you will see it often.

Plans to Prosper

"I know the plans I have for you," declares the Lord,
"plans to prosper you and not to harm you,
plans to give you hope and a future."

JEREMIAH 29:11 NIV

How did this happen? The steering committee had spent so many hours in meetings until the day the social media program was executed. All the work was to ensure that ticket sales would explode. As team leader, Wendy knew this would put her reputation on the map, placing her in demand for any future events. But if it were a big flop, all eyes would be on her as well.

There are many reasons human efforts fail. Through failure we learn that our security is never in our plans. Rather, it's through God's plans that we can trust our futures. He pre-ordained every aspect of our lives. He sees the future and he has gone there ahead of us to prepare the way and to ensure we thrive. His ways are not our ways so even if you don't understand the road bumps along the way, have faith. He created and controls all that he chose for you and has called you to an abundant life in him.

Grace upon Grace

*Make a list of some of the ways God's plan
has interrupted your plan.*

Mind of Christ

"The Helper is the Spirit of truth, whom the world cannot receive, because it does not see Him or know Him; but you know Him because He remains with you and will be in you."

JOHN 14:17 NASB

Ever feel like you are living with information overload? Theories and opinions come at us daily, and we can't even be sure that there is truth to any of them. Which expert is correct, and why did he represent one viewpoint last week and another this week? Yet the world laps it up. People grasp each new opinion and get behind whatever sounds right in the moment.

Even with the Savior of the world standing right in front of him, Pontius Pilate asked, "What is truth?" We cannot understand or see authenticity unless we look with the spiritual eyes of our rebirth. The only truth is spoken in God's Word and confirmed through the Holy Spirit as he convicts our hearts. As Christians, Scripture says we have the mind of Christ. As his Spirit dwells in us, he equips us and verifies our position in him. The Holy Spirit assures us of the accuracy of every single word of Scripture.

Grace upon Grace

Go somewhere quiet and ask the Holy Spirit to speak to you.

In Little or Much

"Blessed are those who trust in the LORD
and have made the LORD their hope and confidence."

JEREMIAH 17:7 NLT

Angela's life had so many ups and downs from new jobs
to no jobs, good health to illness, and friendships that
fell by the wayside due to misunderstandings. These
circumstances caused her to lose sleep and to worry.
She had nowhere to turn in her times of trouble because
Angela's faith was depleted. She was ignoring the true
source of her faith. The cares of this world caused her to
mistrust the one who loved her most.

The Word calls us blessed when we trust in the Lord.
Anyone who has spent dedicated time at the feet of Jesus
would not choose to go anywhere but to him in times of
trial or lack. With the Savior by our side, we flourish even
in the greatest of scarcity. With Jesus on the throne in our
life, the dry spells are filled with refreshment and peace. If
we are serving our King, we put our faith in the one who is
able to bless us more abundantly than we can ever imagine.

Grace upon Grace

*Buy fresh flowers to remind you of how you
can flourish under God's care.*

Trusting God

I am confident of this very thing, that He who began a good work among you will complete it by the day of Christ Jesus.

PHILIPPIANS 1:6 NASB

If you have been onboarded for a new job or given instructions for a DIY project, you know the newness in the situation can have its challenges. Striving to understand can lead to feelings of inadequacy or drowning. You put your best foot forward and hunker down to gain all the knowledge you can to perform your task. Somewhere along the way you start to lose your determination and begin to think about throwing in the towel.

Trusting God to finish what he started is essential to your walk of faith. Hebrews 11 says that without faith it is impossible to please God. If you find your belief in his good work waning, open the Word and ask God to convict your heart of his faithfulness. Pray for confidence that what he says will be accomplished. Even if you continue to struggle, submit yourself to God and he will be faithful even when you are not.

Grace upon Grace

Read Hebrews 11 before you go to bed.

He Provides

"Don't worry about your life, what you will eat or what
you will drink; or about your body, what you will wear.
Isn't life more than food and the body more than clothing?
Consider the birds of the sky: They don't sow or reap or
gather into barns, yet your heavenly Father feeds them.
Aren't you worth more than they?"

MATTHEW 6:25-26 CSB

Voices were raised in frustration as the couple discussed last
month's bills. Roger was stressed out over all the money being
spent and Sophie shed tears over his anger. She confessed
it was hard to watch others with so much when they had to
stick to such a tight budget. Sometimes she overcompensated
for the lack by splurging on something that would lift her
mood. He relented his anger and lovingly reminded Sophie
that life was much more than material things.

Scripture tells us not to be concerned for the things we
truly need because they will be provided by our loving
heavenly Father. If you have found yourself ruminating
over what you don't have, look at what you do. Trust God to
give you what will mature you in faith. He'll always provide
what you need.

Grace upon Grace

*Make a meal using only ingredients
already available in your kitchen.*

Call on Him

I called on the LORD, who is worthy of praise,
and he saved me from my enemies.

PSALM 18:3 NLT

All Bette did was share her thoughts and it stirred up a firestorm amongst the group of women she called her friends. She had prayed and felt that the Lord wanted her to speak out. Immediately the women reprimanded her for even thinking such a thing. It felt like a full-on attack and all Bette wanted to do was retract her comments and run from the room. She sat there feeling like an outcast when suddenly Rose spoke up. This ally had Scripture to back up what Bette had shared and that quickly silenced the others.

When God moves us to speak it won't always be met with approval. There's often a doubter present who wants to challenge others, especially when they don't know the truth themselves. God always supports those who honor and obey his leading. Pray for protection over your words and for the Spirit's leading over whatever you say. Praise him that he hears you and answers when you call. As you obey, he will defend you.

Grace upon Grace

Thank someone who defended you recently.

Riches in Christ

My God will supply all your needs
according to his riches in glory in Christ Jesus.

PHILIPPIANS 4:19 CSB

As Lisa and her kids loaded the trunk with the bags of groceries, she wondered if they had forgotten anything. They started home knowing they could always return to the store for whatever they missed. When they left the parking lot, they saw a woman and a small child sitting on the curb with a sign asking for food. Feeling compelled, Lisa and the kids stopped and shared their groceries with her. Through her tears the woman thanked them, acknowledging that she saw Jesus through their actions.

The Lord is Jehovah-Jireh, the God who provides. Scripture says he will supply our needs and he is pleased when we do the same for others. Today's verse applies to our needs but also to facilitating the development of the fruits of the Spirit. The gifts of wisdom, discernment, encouragement, prophecy, and teaching are just a few of the riches God has for us in Christ. He will always take care of our daily necessities. His desire is to endow us with spiritual growth that glorifies his name.

Grace upon Grace

Give to someone in need whether in person or online.

Give It to Jesus

Out of my distress I called on the LORD:
the LORD answered me and set me free.
The LORD is on my side; I will not fear.
What can man do to me?

PSALM 118:5-6 ESV

Worrying is like a vise squeezing the life out of you. You imagine all the ways that something can go wrong. Nothing bad has happened, but your anxiety is making you live like it already has. In a world filled with anger, people fight to defend themselves. If actually wronged, they can take it out on others in horrific ways. We become programmed to consistently look over our shoulders, frightened that someone will cause us to suffer great harm.

If we would only give it to Jesus, trusting him that all we have and everything we are is controlled by his design. When dread strikes, we should go immediately to God, calling out to him for comfort and answers that only he can give. Nothing happens to us that does not pass through his approval first. You can be certain that he is always by your side and will not allow you to be overcome.

Grace upon Grace

Turn on worship music and battle anxiety with your praise.

Seek Him Always

"Seek the Kingdom of God above all else, and live righteously, and he will give you everything you need."

MATTHEW 6:33 NLT

We all have times when the load is heavier than other times. We might be booked solid such that we can barely catch a breath. It's only Monday and you feel like you've put too many hours of work into a single morning. Stress presses in. How will everything get done? Just when your worry has hit a fever pitch, you notice your Bible on the table. Suddenly you realize that if you would seek God first and foremost, your cares would dissipate.

We need to remember that God has all the answers. We are never going to change anything by fretting about it. Remember the basics—seek the Lord first and live an upright life; he will take care of the rest. If you spend all day sweating over what might happen, you have wasted precious hours. Instead, pick up that Bible, say a prayer, and put today to good use by trusting in Jesus.

Grace upon Grace

Clean out a junk drawer or shelf
and see if you find something useful.

Completion

He will complete what he appoints for me,
and many such things are in his mind.

JOB 23:14 ESV

There were so many things April wanted to accomplish in
her life. There were dreams to pursue and goals to reach
alongside those everyday tasks that demanded her time
and attention. She decided to go for the gusto. She'd get that
new job, lose the weight, and finish that big project that had
been sitting half done for months. Even still, April's best
laid plans didn't go as she had planned.

Do you know what God is doing right now? He is thinking
about you. The Bible says he will never leave us or forsake
us. The Word says that our God opens doors that no man
can shut and shuts those no man can open. He will never
stop short of fulfilling his purpose for you. Trust him, cease
striving, and believe his good will for you.

Grace upon Grace

*Write out some steps you need to take
to accomplish a task God has given you.*

Not Broken

The LORD is near to the brokenhearted
And saves those who are crushed in spirit.

PSALM 34:18 NASB

As the news came in, each detail caused Viv's heart to break. She didn't feel it at first because it was such a shock, but as she began to process what happened, she detected a deep pain in her chest. It grew worse, and with each sob Viv was certain she would never come back from this. Then warmth entered her. It had always been there, but now she sensed it. A palpable peace Viv didn't even understand had entered her soul.

There is an all-encompassing Spirit that surrounds us continually. We have a God who comforts us in the least or most tragic of circumstances. He hides us under his wing and consoles us with the greatest of compassion as we cry. If you haven't noticed how close he is, stop and whisper a prayer. There, you'll find him. He will mercifully mend the brokenhearted and give hope for the future. He will save and repair, making beauty out of the ashes.

Grace upon Grace

Extend grace and try to repair a broken relationship.

Confrontations

If anyone has caused grief, he has not grieved me, but all of you to some extent—not to be too severe. This punishment which was inflicted by the majority is sufficient for such a man, so that, on the contrary, you ought rather to forgive and comfort him, lest perhaps such a one be swallowed up with too much sorrow.

2 CORINTHIANS 2:5-7 NKJV

"Lord, I know Jan has to be confronted," prayed Phillipa, the women's ministry leader. "Scripture is clear on the matter." She had vacillated for weeks since she had become aware of Jan's wrongdoings and offenses. Knowing she had to seek the Lord and have the right motives in her heart before she spoke to Jan, Phillipa waited for the Spirit's leading. When the Lord said go, she went in humility and with authority.

Church discipline is a tough subject and one that tends to get avoided. We can't pick and choose what we want to accept in God's Word so we must adhere to it all. Whether we are addressing the wrongdoing or are caught in sin, we must obey God's strategy for restoration. If we are called to correct another, we must do it in love. If we being corrected, we should show gratitude that someone cared enough to step in.

Grace upon Grace

Before you correct someone,
fill your heart with love for them.

Suffering

What we suffer now is nothing
compared to the glory he will reveal to us later.

ROMANS 8:18 NLT

It was a day for throwing a party but there would be no balloons, no cake, and no presents, because it was a pity party. "Where are you God?" Shara shouted. As the words left her mouth, a truth hit her heart. He was right there; he had never left. Even though she might not believe it at this point, everything Shara was experiencing was allowed in order to make her into the likeness of the Son. She took a breath, stopped her questioning, and said to herself, "He's here. He loves me and he will always do what is best for me."

The suffering we face in life is a work in progress that will someday birth a masterpiece of glory. We may not understand now, but once we are in heaven, we will see the beauty in the pain and the transformation it wrought. Someday when we look into the eyes of Jesus, we will see that our endurance and victory brought honor to his name.

Grace upon Grace

Thank Jesus for enduring the suffering
that brought you salvation.

Life is No Game

"When you pass through the waters, I will be with you;
and through the rivers, they shall not overwhelm you;
when you walk through fire you shall not be burned,
and the flame shall not consume you."

ISAIAH 43:2 ESV

The character on screen faced the most dangerous of all the situations in the game. As Hallie toggled the controller, she sent the warrior through floods, volcanos, and straight toward the giant opponent. Somehow the onscreen player repeatedly skated through the jaws of death to live another day. When Hallie was asked how the digital guy did it, she said, "Because I control where he goes and what the outcome will be."

We would never compare the life God has given us to a video game, but it's an interesting thought. In a game, the automated character has no choice of his own, but we have free will. We can choose to walk defiantly into sin, but it will ultimately lead to death. We don't get another life like the player in the game. Eternity will be determined. Today, let's submit and confess any trespass and acknowledge our need for God.

Grace upon Grace

Tell someone how God graciously saved you from harm.

February

God saved you by his grace
when you believed.
And you can't take credit for this;
it is a gift from God.

EPHESIANS 2:8 NLT

Good Shepherd

Even though I walk through the darkest valley,
I will fear no evil, for you are with me;
your rod and your staff, they comfort me.

PSALM 23:4 NIV

Earlier, Carly had tried to find a parking spot closer to the building where the meeting would be. None were to be found. When the meeting wrapped up, she had to walk the distance back to the car in the unfamiliar neighborhood. Carly nervously kept watch over her surroundings as she walked. If only she had a co-worker who could accompany her, but they had all found spaces in front of the building. All she wanted was to get to her car and lock the door.

As Christ followers, we are never alone, not even in the most dangerous of situations. We have a Good Shepherd who will wield his rod to protect us from harm. He may also use it to remind us to obey. His staff guides us on the right path. If we choose to wander, he uses it to gently pull us back in. It draws us to his side where he woos us to intimacy with him. We are blessed with a Good Shepherd who uses the instruments at his disposal to keep us safely close and in his care.

Grace upon Grace

*Walk a path nearby and thank God for his grace
that allows you to return to him.*

Rejoicing in Trials

In this you greatly rejoice, even though now for a little while,
if necessary, you have been distressed by various trials, so
that the proof of your faith, being more precious than gold
which perishes though tested by fire, may be found to result
in praise, glory, and honor at the revelation of Jesus Christ.

1 PETER 1:6-7 NASB

There are days when you feel like you can't do anything
right. No matter what you throw at the wall, nothing sticks.
Each time you think things are about to get better, they
don't. With each perceived failure you sink deeper into the
negative emotions, and your hope dissipates. Once again
you are trying to understand why things just aren't working
out on your own. Realization sets in, and you stop and
humbly drop to your knees.

We can get so weary from our daily trials that we lose our
spiritual sense. It's a negative path we start to follow if we
listen intently to our battered emotions. What if, instead,
we start praising God? His Word tells us why we will face
trials. It is to prove our faith and refine our character. The
result is victory through Christ.

Grace upon Grace

*As you lay down to sleep, praise God
for the trials he has brought you through.*

Self-Control

Blessed is the one who endures trials, because when he has stood the test he will receive the crown of life that God has promised to those who love him.

JAMES 1:12 CSB

Mila had pictures all over the refrigerator of the new clothes she wanted to fit. The problem was that as she gazed at the trendy attire, she thought about that cheesecake inside the fridge. Just one bite, right? There couldn't be many calories in just one taste. Mila gingerly opened the door, convincing herself that she would have enough self-control. After she finished the entire slice, however, she sunk into discouragement again. She was now even further away from her desired goal.

"Life is short, so eat dessert first," right? If we apply that mantra to all our struggles with temptation, we will lose the battle. We are strengthened by believing all that Scripture has to say. If we prevail over a life of sin, we will receive an eternal crown that exists forever. Don't let your failures keep you from experiencing what God has promised to those who love him.

Grace upon Grace

Stop and ask God for help when you need the power to be victorious in Christ.

Intercession

In a similar way, the Holy Spirit takes hold of us in our
human frailty to empower us in our weakness.

ROMANS 8:26 TPT

Have you ever been asked to help someone in their time
of need, yet you felt completely unequipped? Maybe it was
you who required assistance, but you thought you might
be inconveniencing the other person. Whether it's you or
someone else who has an urgent need, making an appeal
for help can be hindered by the fear of being a burden. This
leaves us stuck and without a solution.

As believers, we have the Holy Spirit as our constant
companion and helper. One of the most incredible ways
he aids us is through our prayers. If our hearts are heavy,
the words struggle to come. We can trust that in those
times, the Spirit is interceding in ways that are touching
the very throne of God. There's no way we can ever pray
with the same power that the Spirit has on our behalf. Be at
peace, offer praise, and rejoice that your prayers are being
represented supernaturally. The Holy Spirit prays with a
depth of spiritual cries that are beyond our ability.

Grace upon Grace

*Pray for the Holy Spirit to accomplish
breakthrough for a friend.*

Overdoing It

Let us not grow weary of doing good,
for in due season we will reap,
if we do not give up.

GALATIANS 6:9 ESV

Overwhelmed, stressed, and discouraged—do any of these describe you? It's easy in this life to want to do it all and hopefully avoiding FOMO (fear of missing out). We have dreams and goals. We want to be in the right place at the right time. We don't want to risk missing that one event that might open a door. We overcommit and, in the process, become so ragged we can't keep up.

So, should we quit? No way! Scripture tells us not to grow weary in doing good, are we only involved in good? Do we pray and ask for God's blessing before we start committing? If not, we will find ourselves saying yes to everything and struggling with all those overwhelmed and discouraged feelings. We must involve God's will in every decision we make so we can serve with excellence.

Grace upon Grace

*Look at your calendar and ask God
what he wants you to continue or quit.*

Coming Glory

Rejoice as you share in the sufferings of Christ, so that you may also rejoice with great joy when his glory is revealed.

1 PETER 4:13 CSB

Sara learned early on that she was different. At the age of twenty-two, she had suffered surgery after surgery for twenty years. Pain was her daily companion. It was hard to understand and excruciating to watch for those who loved her. Yet, the most amazing thing was Sara's attitude of joy. She knew that the trial she endured was nothing compared to the one her Savior suffered on her behalf. If he could face the cross for her, she would carry hers for him. She found the strength to continue knowing that one day, he would welcome her into his arms and say, "Well done, good and faithful servant."

We may never face difficulties like Sara, but Jesus assured us we would have troubles. Will we suffer well, bearing in mind what Christ did for us? May we all keep our eyes on the reward of heaven and the promise of eternity, knowing that who we have believed is faithful.

Grace upon Grace

Thank Jesus for his grace that gives you the promise of eternity.

Doing It Right

"Whoever hears these sayings of Mine, and does them,
I will liken him to a wise man who built his house on the
rock: and the rain descended, the floods came, and the
winds blew and beat on that house; and it did not fall,
for it was founded on the rock."

MATTHEW 7:24-25 NKJV

Every teen in the class had been given the same
assignment. They had detailed instructions, mathematical
measurements, and safety procedures in order to perform
the science experiment properly. Most students followed
the guidelines carefully. Those who were struggling asked
the teacher for assistance. Yet there was always one student
who wasn't paying attention. Soon the air filled with an
odious smell that sent everyone running from the room.

When a fool acts in error it is often on display for everyone
to see. Great damage can be done when tasks are performed
in haste or without adequate caution. The Bible tells us we
are not merely to read or listen to God's Word, but we are to
carry out its teachings to the letter. When we understand,
memorize, and obey Scripture we will have a strong and
sturdy structure as the basis for what we believe.

Grace upon Grace

Pick a life verse that speaks to you and memorize it.

Ironclad Promise

Don't throw away your confidence,
which has a great reward.

HEBREWS 10:35 CSB

Jozie wanted to give up. She had repeatedly tried to sew some pieces together to create a beautiful blouse, but it was nothing like her mother's blouse. Her mom tried to teach her how to sew because it would benefit her for the rest of her life. Whether Jozie did it for fun or as a job, she would have an ability that she could utilize forever. Jozie told her mom about her struggles, and she graciously stepped in to help. Mom explained and guided Jozie through each step until she completed her project.

Before we were ever born, God knew us. He preordained our existence, purposing every day. Without him, we are not capable of taking a breath. Though we are dust, he calls us his children. He loves us with everlasting love. He guaranteed with the blood of Jesus that those who know him will spend eternity in heaven with him. He will complete all he has planned for you and that is an iron-clad promise.

Grace upon Grace

*When you see a product guarantee,
remember God's gracious promise of eternity.*

No Condemnation

There is now no condemnation
for those who are in Christ Jesus.

ROMANS 8:1 NIV

Brian had told his sister a million times to stay out of his room and never touch his stuff. Janie asked ad nauseam about the intricate model heart he had built for his biology class. She just wanted to touch it once. Receiving a firm no, Janie waited until Brian drove off to meet friends. She snuck into his room and ran her fingers gingerly across the plastic replica. As she turned to leave, her long hair swooshed past the heart and knocked it off its mount, shattering it.

Can you imagine Brian's reaction when he returned and found his model in a million pieces? Or can you feel Janie's tears as she blames herself for her foolishness? Both were assuredly at odds and devastated. For those of us in Christ, we can be certain that no matter how serious the sin, if we confess it, there is immediate absolution. Once forgiven, God forgets the wrongs committed. All he sees is the beauty of a heart surrendered to him, repentant and ready with renewed dedication to follow and obey.

Grace upon Grace

*Quickly confess any sin you currently have
and know God's grace will immediately cover it.*

Sharing Mercy

All praise to God, the Father of our Lord Jesus Christ.
God is our merciful Father and the source of all comfort.
He comforts us in all our troubles so that we can comfort
others. When they are troubled, we will be able to give
them the same comfort God has given us.

2 CORINTHIANS 1:3-4 NLT

When Isobel, the young widow, heard that her neighbor
had just lost her husband, a flood of emotions ran through
her. It was as if that death of her husband was happening
all over again. The sudden tragic news, the shock, and the
initial denial seared her heart like an open wound. Even
though it had been years now, it seemed as though it was
yesterday. Isobel knew she must go to her neighbor who
was suffering as she had. She knew she could give comfort
to her in her time of loss.

God is a loving Father who understands our pain. He sees
what's coming before we do, and in his mercy, he provides
people to minister to us. Often those people have walked
similar paths before us and can touch our hearts in ways no
one else could. Open your heart and experiences to others in
order to bless and bring peace to them in their time of sorrow.

Grace upon Grace

Reach out to someone needing comfort.

Short-Lived Anger

His anger lasts only a moment,
but his favor, a lifetime.

PSALM 30:5 CSB

Leanna and Mario did something they promised they would never do as a couple—they went to bed angry. Mario had dug his heels in leaving Leanna with no choice. Deep in anger and unable to nod off, she cried herself to sleep while he slept soundly. At the sun's rising they awoke, realizing they couldn't even remember why the fight started. Desiring to make things right regardless of who bore the greater guilt, he apologized and embraced her.

The Bible warns us against becoming enraged. There are many times, however, that the Lord experienced times of anger with the Israelites. We can be certain that he was justified in his emotions for he is a righteous God. Where Scripture speaks of his outrage, it clearly states that his anger was short-lived. His desire is not to rebuke but to shower his unfailing love into the lives of his children.

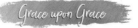

Grace upon Grace

Do not let anger take root in your heart.

Look Up

Why are you cast down, O my soul?
And why are you disquieted within me?
Hope in God;
For I shall yet praise Him,
The help of my countenance and my God.

PSALM 42:11 NKJV

When Jennie considered the reality of things—the world and all its uncertainty—she found herself experiencing a heaviness in her chest. Worry crouched at her side wanting to engulf her with unfounded fears from unvetted news reports. Events Jennie had planned to attend now made her worry about what might happen at a public gathering. Anxiety tempted her to roll up in a ball, hide her face, and retreat from anything outside her front door.

It's true. We live in an unstable world, but hasn't it truthfully been that way since the days of Adam and Eve? There's nothing new under the sun. Man has always dealt with evil. Yet for those who have faith in God, there's hope; his name is Jesus. We can rejoice, have peace, and live fearlessly because God is at our side. Look up in praise, for your Redeemer is always nearby!

Grace upon Grace

Rebuke fear and choose to praise the Lord, your Redeemer.

Our Shelter

The one who lives under the protection of the Most High
dwells in the shadow of the Almighty.

PSALM 91:1 CSB

It can be easy to take the roof over our heads for granted.
We trust it to be there every morning when we wake up.
Home can seem like our constant, reliable haven. When
storms come it shelters us. If the temperatures rise, we can
find a quiet, cool spot to reside. It's a comfort to know we
have a place to call our own where we can rest, retreat, and
feel safe.

When we think of the Almighty, do we get such a sense of
comfort? Do we think of him first every morning when
we awaken? Are we actively seeking to stay close to him?
Do we consider God to be our one true home? A roof can
cave in, but God never lets us down. Our home could be
flattened by a natural disaster, but God is the lifter of our
heads. Don't put your trust in earthly structures. Place your
faith in God alone. Be purposeful in your daily life to reside
in the shadow of his shelter, close to his heart, and filled
with his Spirit.

Grace upon Grace

Tell Jesus how he is your everything.

Pray Before Speaking

An offended friend is harder to win back
than a fortified city.
Arguments separate friends like a gate locked with bars.

PROVERBS 18:19 NLT

Lou, Felicity, and Ruby were dear friends, and all three believed they could be transparent with each other. Apparently, that was not the case, for Lou and Ruby were taking sides against Felicity. It didn't seem as if they would ever reconcile. The constructive criticism that Felicity offered to Ruby was not taken well. How dare Lou defend Ruby, who was obviously at fault? Because Felicity was already deeply offended by Ruby in the first place, when Lou sided with her over Felicity, it was just heaping insult upon insult.

Scripture tells us that offense is a tough emotion to heal. It strikes our heart with a sledgehammer. If a friend is in the wrong and must be confronted, humility and grace are essential. We are to correct within the body, but if we don't do it with the Holy Spirit's leading and the truth of God's Word, we do more harm than good. Before you speak, spend time in prayer, check your own heart, and move forward with godly intent.

Grace upon Grace

*Always pause and pray for the Holy Spirit to lead you
before confronting a friend.*

The Gospel

"Go therefore and make disciples of all nations, baptizing them in the name of the Father and of the Son and of the Holy Spirit, teaching them to observe all that I have commanded you."

MATTHEW 28:19 ESV

MaryAnne was given one job—just one task—and she spent time doing everything but that simple thing. So many distractions lead her away from the goal. There were daily responsibilities, lifetime goals, and the steps required to reach her planned future. However, when night came and she lay in bed, there was a nagging thought that she had ignored something important. MaryAnne hadn't spoken of the one thing that could save her loved ones and friends from an eternity spent outside of the presence of God.

This verse should be a wake-up call for all of us. We plan our lives; we make our dream boards and put our might into reaching those targets. Yet, as believers in Christ, we know that he gave us one duty that ranks above all others. We're to share the gospel and disciple those who choose to follow Jesus. How many of us wake up each day determined to fulfill that calling? If we're not sharing, why not?

Grace upon Grace

Pray for the opportunity to share the good news of salvation with someone.

His Goodness

We know that God causes all things to work together for good to those who love God, to those who are called according to His purpose.

ROMANS 8:28 NASB

You try to decide all the pros and cons of your chosen path. All the what ifs keep circling around in your mind. Then there are the grandiose daydreams of glorious achievements if you succeed. Yet you conclude that, on your own, you don't have the confidence to take that step of faith. Too many unknowns make you skittish and the possible consequences are too dire to risk. Still, you vacillate, and you can't seem to decide.

Aren't you thankful that as believers in Christ, Scripture proves we're not the originator of our best-life plan, nor are we the ones who will bring it to fruition? The Word tells us that God works for our good in all things and if we'll only trust, submit and seek his will, we have this guarantee.

Grace upon Grace

Find a comfy chair to sit and ponder God's goodness to you.

Pray About Anxiety

Do not be anxious about anything, but in every situation,
by prayer and petition, with thanksgiving, present your
requests to God. And the peace of God, which transcends
all understanding, will guard your hearts and your minds
in Christ Jesus.

PHILIPPIANS 4:6-7 NIV

We are overly bombarded with news of world events and
stress of personal issues. In the moment, we take it all in
and let it weigh down our soul. We start to ponder what we
could do to change situations or affect outcomes. Should we
write to our senators or live in fear at the abundance of evil?
While one is proactive, the other is apt to make us curl up
in the fetal position.

The answer to these problems is in today's verse. First, go
to God in grateful prayer. Let your anxiety dissipate as
you recount his character. He is faithful. Your concern is
not a surprise to him. He wants to provide peace beyond
comprehension. Let your thoughts be protected by his
promises. Even in an uncertain future, you can trust who
you believe in.

Grace upon Grace

*Silence your anxious thoughts by praying about
whatever is causing you anxiety.*

Confidence Through Christ

Let's approach the throne of grace with confidence,
so that we may receive mercy and find grace for help
at the time of our need.

HEBREWS 4:16 NASB

Emma spent a lot of time practicing for her big presentation.
She stood in front of the mirror reworking her approach
many times. She tried not to think negatively or make any
comments about the way she looked but to stick to the crux
of her presentation. She needed to make the point with
conviction, not draw unnecessary attention to herself. Her
end goal was to gain enough interest from people in order
to get the support necessary to move forward with her ideas.
On the day of her big pitch Emma gave herself a pep talk,
believing her presentation would succeed.

Aren't you thankful that you have access to the throne of
God through the torn veil? Due to Christ's work on the
cross, you can go anytime of the day or night with the full
assurance that you will be heard. We can be confident that
our prayers will be answered with his extravagant, attentive
mercy and grace.

Grace upon Grace

*Close your eyes and picture God the Father on the
throne of grace beckoning you to come near to him.*

Motive of the Heart

This is the confidence that we have toward him,
that if we ask anything according to his will he hears us.

1 JOHN 5:14 ESV

It's easy to get caught up in the desire for material things, whether it is clothing, furniture, or a vacation home. There are generous Christians who share their valued possessions with those in need. For example, if they own a cabin on the lake, they will offer it to families for their enjoyment. We are wise to show humility and generosity with the blessings God gives us.

When we ask God for something in prayer, we should first seek to understand the reasons we are asking. Is it to use in service to others or only for our own pleasure? Does it show the love of God and further his kingdom? If it pertains to his will regarding how and where we serve Him, is there anything selfish in it or is it in full surrender? God loves to give his children good gifts, but he particularly smiles on a heart that asks with the intention of bringing glory to his name.

Grace upon Grace

*Consider the motives of your heart
with the requests you bring to God.*

On Behalf of Others

Confess your sins to each other and pray for each other so
that you may be healed. The earnest prayer of a righteous
person has great power and produces wonderful results.

JAMES 5:16 NLT

At times, we struggle with sin that is ingrained in our
behavior. Hard as we try, we continually revisit it. We
acknowledge we have fallen again, and discouragement
sets in. It is the awareness of the difficulty that moves us to
understand we need an ally to join us in the fight. Scripture
says that we are to bear one another's burdens. We must
do that with compassion, being aware not to engage in sin
ourselves. Remember what Christ has forgiven you of and
enter into fervent prayer with grace.

If you are entrusted with another's battle, speak in the
power of the Holy Spirit and with the love of Jesus. It is
not an easy decision to make: to bear the depths of one's
soul. Seek wisdom as you pray and know that you have
been chosen to be a prayer warrior through whom God is
working.

Grace upon Grace

*Whenever you minister to others, ask for wisdom,
guidance, and love from the Holy Spirit.*

Controlling Your Temper

The discretion of a man makes him slow to anger,
And his glory is to overlook a transgression.

PROVERBS 19:11 NKJV

Barb got cut off in traffic, and she had the urge to respond inappropriately. Then she noticed the Jesus sticker in her back window and decided it would be better to let it go. Even something as small as a sticker can help a believer choose to exhibit good behavior. When Barb arrived home, she saw that her kids had not followed through on their chores. Why don't they keep their responsibilities? Then she noticed a note on the counter. She was supposed to help a friend out today and had completely forgotten. Humbled, Barb showed her kids the grace she hoped her neglected friend would show her.

The Bible says many things about those who are quick to anger. The Word describes these people as a fool, an evildoer, the unrighteous, or one who stirs up strife. Those who resist taking offense and overlook another's wrongdoing are called wise, prudent, loving, and compassionate. We honor God when we avoid anger and forgive quickly when wronged.

Grace upon Grace

When tempted to lose your temper,
offer grace and mercy instead.

Green-Eyed Monster

Wherever jealousy and selfishness are uncovered, you will also find many troubles and every kind of meanness.

JAMES 3:16 TPT

The neighborhood friends just couldn't stand to hear one more word about Lila's upcoming vacation. She described it in detail—the high-end resort, the fabulous amenities, the posh services that would be at her beck and call. They tried to change the subject whenever Lila brought it up, but somehow, she found ways to keep talking about it. The green-eyed monster was alive and well within the neighborhood as the happy traveler monopolized the days before her trip.

Who was wrong in this scenario? Truthfully, Lila and the other women in the neighborhood were all at fault. The braggart had no sympathy for her friends who could not afford such a treat. Her sharing was thoughtless and egotistical. The jealous women were also wrong since they could not be happy for their friend without being bitter about their own lives. We must look to the needs, feelings, and welfare of others to best consider those around us. Putting others' feelings first exemplifies the heart of Jesus.

Grace upon Grace

Examine your words before sharing anything that would cause another jealousy.

Love Your Neighbor

"Do not seek revenge or bear a grudge against anyone
among your people, but love your neighbor as yourself.
I am the LORD."

LEVITICUS 19:18 NIV

The two families had lived next door to each other for
twenty years and had spent countless hours socializing.
Lately, however, they were at odds. The fence needed to
be replaced and although the responsibility truthfully
belonged to both the Leonards and the Smiths, James
Leonard was adamant that the property line was positioned
such that the fence was not on his land. Even if they
could agree to share the cost, James wanted to choose the
inexpensive route, and Tim Smith wanted top-of-the-line
materials. It got to the point where they avoided each other
and that degraded their relationship even further.

We can destroy relationships over such silly things. There's
a reason God went to such lengths in Scripture to describe
how we are to love and care for one another. We are
instructed to have the same attitude Jesus had. We need to
humble ourselves for the good of others, going to all lengths
to live together in peace.

Grace upon Grace

Think of someone's needs that you can place ahead of your own.

Handling Insults

He did not retaliate when he was insulted, nor threaten revenge when he suffered. He left his case in the hands of God, who always judges fairly.

1 PETER 2:23 NLT

Zane was calm and silent throughout the barrage of verbal attacks. A big deal had been lost and even though it was not his fault, his boss decided he deserved the blame. Co-workers stood by, speechless at the lack of grace exhibited by their boss but even more amazed at Zane's composure. And Zane's behavior solidified their admiration. They knew him as a hard worker and an honest man. This treatment of him was unwarranted, yet he remained respectful.

When Jesus was crucified, he was silent. Although he endured physical abuse, verbal jabs, and tremendous torture, he did not retaliate. When they yelled for the notorious prisoner, Barabbas, to be released rather than Jesus, he didn't demand justice. When they nailed him to the cross, he didn't fight them. He trusted his life to God. We will never suffer like he did, but if insults do come, don't seek vengeance. Respond as Jesus would with trust in God.

Grace upon Grace

Think about the last time you were insulted and how you could have responded differently.

Human Knowledge

The Jews ask for signs and the Greeks seek wisdom, but we preach Christ crucified, a stumbling block to the Jews and foolishness to the Gentiles.

1 CORINTHIANS 1:22-23 CSB

Professor Young just would not take anyone's word for anything. He had always been a doubter, and it was in his nature to question everything that wasn't black and white. If someone proposed a theory, he insisted they prove it with facts. Even the most learned of men with multiple degrees couldn't convince him. In the long run, the professor's lack of trust made him too difficult to deal with. He was left friendless within his own narrow scope of knowledge which fell short of some of life's most important insights.

When men seek human knowledge, they miss the mystery of God. If you've ever heard anyone say that the gospel is too simple, you have met a person who believes their thoughts are above God's, and that their understanding is greater. We'll never attain our Lord's intelligence, and we won't comprehend everything on this side of heaven. We must trust what we don't adequately perceive because we believe in the true identity of our God.

Grace upon Grace

Think of who you can go to with spiritual questions.

Loving Well

Love suffers long and is kind; love does not envy; love does not parade itself, is not puffed up; does not behave rudely, does not seek its own, is not provoked, thinks no evil.

1 Corinthians 13:4-5 NKJV

It was a lovely event, but as Rhoda looked around the room, she saw a couple of women she knew. Rhoda noticed they dressed in expensive clothes and obviously could afford spa days. The comparison between herself and these two was killing her—they weren't very nice and had offended her several times! Maybe if she emphasized some of the good bits about her own life, she could elevate herself. Or she could mention some of the bad behavior exhibited by these two. After all, they had hurt her and should definitely be set straight.

We are emotional beings, and we tend to wear our feelings on our sleeves. When we compare ourselves to others, we try to justify our own goodness, which only results in poor behavior. The only way we can love well is to forgive and care with the heart of Jesus. Spend time at his feet, commit his Word to memory, and pray that the power of the Holy Spirit will cause others to see Jesus by the way you live.

Grace upon Grace

Stop comparison in its tracks and ask God to help you love like Jesus, full of grace.

The Cornerstone

To you who believe, this stone is precious. But to those
who do not believe, "The stone the builders rejected has
become the cornerstone," and, "A stone that causes people
to stumble and a rock that makes them fall." They stumble
because they disobey the message—which is also what they
were destined for.

1 PETER 2:7-8 NIV

Some people search for truth and concoct their own beliefs
out of theologies that best suit how they want to live.
This leaves them with a life of fantasy that fits with their
momentary whims. It justifies their actions and their false
beliefs. Ignoring God's cornerstone will only lead to God's
judgment. There is but one truth and that is Jesus Christ.
His salvation offered for us through his sacrifice on the
cross is the precious cornerstone.

Are there areas of your life where you are ignoring what is
righteous and true, replacing it with your own ideals? The
time on this earth is short and eternity is everlasting. Don't
ignore the precious stone that was crushed on your behalf.
Surrender to him and live solely in service to him. Find
your joy and purpose in all that he is.

Grace upon Grace

*Find a stone to act as a visual reminder of Christ,
the cornerstone.*

Guarding your Conscience

Because of this, I always try to maintain a clear conscience before God and all people.

ACTS 24:16 NLT

Anita had a deep aversion to explaining her poor choices or wrongdoings to anyone. It was a great inhibitor for her behavior, and it caused her to carefully watch how she responded in tenuous situations. She wanted to treat people with kindness. She prayed she would grow in Jesus and become someone who would always step in to help when needed. Anita had a longing and a desire to love deeply and be known as trustworthy. She wisely considered her motives and guarded her conscience.

We can't expect good character to just materialize. We must work at it, pray for it, and study the Scriptures. God instructs us on how to mature in Christ. We must take our eyes off this world and have a heavenly perspective. There needs to be a consistent cognitive thought process that keeps a check on how we live, speak, and carry ourselves. Aim high and commit fully, for you represent the only true hope of salvation.

Grace upon Grace

Ask an elderly person or single parent how you can help them.

March

Let us then with confidence
draw near to the throne of grace,
that we may receive mercy and find
grace to help in time of need.

HEBREWS 4:16 ESV

Spiritual Muscles

They go from strength to strength,
till each appears before God in Zion.

PSALM 84:7 NIV

We live in a culture obsessed with image and improvement. Gyms and health spas populate our cities which are full of people seeking their best forms. Webinars are held on every new idea. TED Talks advise how to further your career and win the most coveted positions. Books are written on your best life and how to achieve it. To gain what we desire most we must make our own way and succeed at all costs.

Life is not for the fainthearted. We struggle with ups and downs. It's challenging to navigate our time on earth. The only way to live the life that Jesus intended and to mature in our walk with him is to be yoked to him. Pursue him relentlessly. Love him single-mindedly. Ask him to give you spiritual muscles, a mind of wisdom, and discernment so that you can maneuver with the power of the Holy Spirit. Then when you arrive at the throne you will hear, "Well done."

Grace upon Grace

*Do a spiritual workout today with time in prayer
and in the Word.*

To Be Forgiven

Make allowance for each other's faults and forgive anyone who offends you. Remember, the Lord forgave you, so you must forgive others.

COLOSSIANS 3:13 NLT

It was like a knife to the heart. Tina and Beth had been best friends and had shared everything, but this time Tina spoke out of turn. Beth tried to process Tina's verbal attack. She tried to understand the root of her rude words. Maybe Tina was hurting and said things without considering the consequences, but bitterness had formed. Beth just didn't understand the reason for the rudeness. This led Beth to decide to remove herself from a beautiful, long-term friendship.

It should be a no-brainer to forgive others when we consider all our sins that Christ has forgiven. However, we are filled with faults and defenses that can overwhelm our spiritual judgment. We need a huge dose of Jesus. It should motivate us that if we don't forgive others, God won't forgive us. The commitment of our hearts and our gratitude for his absolution of us should be all we need to pardon others.

Grace upon Grace

Extend the same grace Christ gave to you to those who have offended you.

Short-lived Anger

Be angry and do not sin. Don't let the sun go down on your anger, and don't give the devil an opportunity.

EPHESIANS 4:26-27 CSB

Neither Henry nor Callie would budge from their positions. When the evening was over, they parted without saying another word. Feelings of discouragement and aggravation emerged. They were both rethinking their relationship. Their own viewpoints on the situation had overridden any spiritual insight. They gave their minds over to the enemy instead of committing the situation to Christ with humility and grace.

We can become self-absorbed when we want to be right. We let anger override our hearts and minds, and then become determined not to compromise. Scripture is clear on this; we are standing in the wrong camp when we allow our fury to linger. Satan has a heyday with our emotions if we are stubborn, and God's favor cannot thrive when we give way to embittered feelings. It is sin to reside in our rage. Obey God's Word and do not give way to anger. Forgive as God has forgiven you.

Grace upon Grace

Humble yourself and ask the Lord who you need to graciously forgive.

Unforgiveness

Be kind to one another, tenderhearted,
forgiving one another,
even as God in Christ forgave you.

EPHESIANS 4:32 NKJV

The small Bible study group tended to reject those who
didn't quite meet their standards. When Althea, quite a
lonely woman from the community, tried to join them,
they mentally surveyed her and decided she was not
worthy. Althea tried to figure out how she could persuade
them or please them in order to gain their friendships.
They continued, however, to reject her. She finally gave
up, demoralized; she struggled with an unforgiving heart
toward the tight-knit circle.

Our bad behavior can cause another to fall into the sin
of unforgiveness. The Bible is clear on the need to be
considerate. If you are the one harmed, your spiritual work
is to forgive the wrongdoer. Although what was done to
the woman in the account above was cruel, she is called to
forgive as Jesus has forgiven her. If we turn the other cheek
as God has commanded us to do, we'll receive his approval,
favor, and blessing.

Grace upon Grace

*Consider someone who is struggling to fit in
and find a way to include them.*

Covetousness

Let us not become conceited,
provoking one another,
envying one another.

GALATIANS 5:26 ESV

Laura snuck into the bedroom of her host without being seen and proceeded to rummage through her closet. She had always admired the woman's taste in fashion and coveted her clothing. Believing the party was lively enough for her not to be missed, she began to hold different outfits up in front of a fancy full-length mirror. As she did, the thought that one blouse wouldn't be missed entered her mind. She started to stuff it into her oversized bag right as the host entered the room.

It surprises us what envy can lead someone to do, but it shouldn't. After all, didn't it cause Cain to kill his brother? Stealing one small item may seem like child's play, but to God it is sin. When we believe we are entitled to everything, we behave in ways that are displeasing to God. Pursue thankfulness instead. Live content with the breath he gives you every morning.

Grace upon Grace

*List some things you are grateful for
because of God's grace and provision.*

Maintain Your Testimony

He will keep you safe. But to Israel and Judah he will be a stone that makes people stumble, a rock that makes them fall. And for the people of Jerusalem he will be a trap and a snare.

ISAIAH 8:14 NLT

Leo hung out at the water cooler and was often overheard mocking the beliefs of others. He considered himself a man's man, reliant only upon himself. He found religion to be the opiate of the masses and a fantasy followed by fools. Trish wandered by one day. She was known for declaring God's goodness and her faith in the Savior. Leo taunted her loudly. She knew the protection of her Lord, however, and Leo's berating had no effect on her testimony.

The Lord guards those who are his own. His protection over believers from the hatred of those who don't follow God is constant. When we proceed to share the gospel and our own testimonies, we defeat the deeds of darkness, allowing Christ's light to show through. We must never live in fear of what others think, for many will stumble over the precious cornerstone, Christ, and detest us in the process. We must maintain our testimony, for only God knows who will follow him.

Grace upon Grace

Ask other believers to tell you about the times they were bold in sharing the gospel.

Voice of Wisdom

Understand this: Everyone should be quick to listen, slow
to speak, and slow to anger, for human anger does not
accomplish God's righteousness.

JAMES 1:19-20 CSB

The temptation to give a quick snarky answer was so strong.
The circumstances were really outside Christine's comfort
zone. As she abruptly opened her mouth to reply, Christine
heard a small, still voice say, "Don't!" Scripture started to fill
her mind and she heard the wisdom and discernment of the
Holy Spirit. Despite herself, Christine held back, sensing
immediately the peace and pleasure of God's presence
in her soul. This, for her, was a wonderful, unexpected
blessing as a believer.

As God's beloved, we're to imitate his attitude in all we
do. We should always consider a situation and check the
motives of our hearts before offering our input. Will our
retort carry a sense of anger? Will it be curt in its delivery?
Or will we be the example of Christ in our consideration
of the details, praying over our response. Reacting
immediately without seeking God never has good results.

Grace upon Grace

*Pause and listen for discernment before you respond
in difficult situations.*

Bad Habits

> "Be on your guard! If your brother sins, rebuke him;
> and if he repents, forgive him."
>
> LUKE 17:3 NASB

Trudy didn't even notice the bad habit that had been hers for most of her life. Her home was loosely religious while growing up, so she was never corrected. When her friend, Alberta, lovingly and privately approached her to discuss the curse words she so often used, she bristled at the rebuke. Trudy felt singled out and persecuted. If these words were okay for her parents, why weren't they okay for her? But it wasn't just offensive to Alberta. Her bad language alienated many people. It took several weeks for Trudy to come to terms with the truth, but when she did, she asked Alberta for forgiveness and started on a journey to live more like Jesus.

We must be watchful over our words and our actions. We are accountable for the way we represent our Savior. If we're corrected according to Scripture's guidelines, we should repent and ask for forgiveness. If someone approaches us for forgiveness, we should forgive immediately and welcome back the repentant believer with open arms.

Grace upon Grace

*Create a habit of immediate forgiveness
when someone apologizes.*

Avoiding a Woe

"Things that cause people to stumble are bound to come,
but woe to anyone through whom they come."

LUKE 17:1 NIV

*What's the big deal if the girls engage in a bit of gossip?
Where's the harm?* thought new believer, Alice, to herself.
Then the day came when Alice was the subject of the
conversation. It struck a deep wound in her heart because
the gossiper was Bertie, whom she trusted, and the gossip
was a private issue Alice had confided from her past. It
suddenly hit her that this must be what it felt like to others
when she shared a confidence or embellished a story. Alice
regretted every scandalous word she had ever spoken.

If you read a "woe" in Scripture, you would do well to avoid
whatever causes that woe. Jesus uses it as an exclamation
of grief. To think we would ever cause our Lord anguish or
grief should break our hearts enough to never do it again.
We were already the cause of the nails in his hands and feet.
Let's not do anything else to cause him pain. May we live to
honor, love, and glorify him in everything we do.

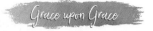

Grace upon Grace

*Ask the Lord to prick your conscience
if you are the reason that someone sins.*

Rebuking the Evil One

Jesus turned to Peter and said, "Get away from me, Satan!
You are a dangerous trap to me. You are seeing things
merely from a human point of view, not from God's."

MATTHEW 16:23 NLT

Nina had been told to keep her distance from the cookie jar
before dinner, yet she just couldn't stop looking at it. Surely
her mama wouldn't mind if she just had one. Then she
remembered the snake in the garden and how he tricked
Eve to doubt God. It was the same trick with her, tempting
her to distrust what her mama had said. That is when Nina
repeated what she had heard her mama say often, "Not
today, Satan!"

It's our responsibility to know God's Word so that
when the evil one lies to us, we can rebuke him. God's
commandments for us are eminently clear. When the devil
speaks a variant of what God said, we need to recognize
it and shut it down immediately. Learn to recognize the
deceiver so that you will be able to hold up your shield of
faith and deflect every one of his arrows.

Grace upon Grace

*Find a verse to use against the deception of Satan
in order to rebuke him.*

Come to Light

"Whoever causes one of these little ones who believe in Me to sin, it would be better for him if a millstone were hung around his neck, and he were drowned in the depth of the sea."

MATTHEW 18:6 NKJV

Allan sat sheepishly outside the principal's office. His concern turned into outright fear when his father came in. He knew this would not go well for him. If only Allan had ignored the older boy, Jeremy, who talked him into that dastardly deed. He knew better, but he just wanted the kids to like him. Jeremy knew he had persuaded Allan to do something wrong, but as he looked on from a safe distance, he was just proud that he had not been caught.

Eventually all ill deeds come to light. Even if it takes until judgment day, all things will be laid bare. It would be best if everyone learned that causing another to sin will be judged. When Jesus says it would be better to die by drowning than to cause another person to sin, he means it. We would do well to take his caution to heart and make sure we never lead anyone else into temptation or sin.

Grace upon Grace

Be responsible with your words and actions,
so you don't cause others to stumble.

Many Times

"If he sins against you seven times in the day, and turns to you seven times, saying, 'I repent,' you must forgive him."

LUKE 17:4 ESV

Nanette was pressing every single nerve her mom had. Every instruction was met with determination to do the exact opposite. Granted, some things Nanette didn't fully understand, but others were just plain defiance. Every time mom doled out the discipline and explained why the correction was needed, Nanette repented. In her weariness, Nanette's mom was tempted not to forgive the little girl until God whispered, "How many times have I forgiven you, my child?"

No matter how many times someone sins against us, it'll never come close to the multitude of transgressions we've committed against our Savior. No matter how many times we forgive, it will never amount to the degree with which God has absolved us with his grace and mercy. We need to be honest about our need to be forgiven, and then freely forgive others. We need to remember that his grace has no limits, and neither should ours.

Grace upon Grace

Never limit the amount of grace you show others because God's grace doesn't have a limit.

Hatred Versus Love

Hatred stirs up quarrels,
but love makes up for all offenses.

PROVERBS 10:12 NLT

The neighbors couldn't understand why Heidi, who lived in the Johnson house, was always picking fights. They had tried to befriend her, but it was becoming harder to be around her. They concluded that there must be some problem or deep-seated hurt that caused her to be so difficult. Finally, someone got to the root of the problem. "Do you really think Heidi understands how much Jesus loves her? Has anyone even told her?" So, they decided one day to tell her the truth about the gospel. Heidi received Christ, and a love flooded her soul, and a transformation began that altered her relationship with her neighbors forever.

Due to some harsh experiences that resulted in some bad choices for the young woman, she had grown to hate herself. Once she came face-to-face with forgiveness and realized how much Jesus loves her regardless of her past, everything changed. She committed her heart to the Savior, believed in his redeeming power, and began to grow into his likeness.

Grace upon Grace

Show love to someone who needs Christ's transforming power.

Forgiving and Forgetting

Whoever conceals an offense promotes love,
but whoever gossips about it separates friends.

PROVERBS 17:9 CSB

The thoughts swirled around in Sue's head throughout
the day and on into the night as she replayed the event of
that day. Her stomach twisted tighter with each sleepless
moment. She tossed and turned as the memory persisted.
Could Sue ever forgive her friend, Annie? Was the
relationship over? Did she want it to end? She certainly
would never allow herself to be treated in such a way again.
The more Sue reviewed the matter, the more she felt the
distaste of it. She wondered how Annie was doing with it
all. She thought about how much she would miss her if this
were not resolved.

Forgiving and forgetting while moving forward with a
bad memory is difficult. Have you ever wondered how
God does it? He's forgiven the entire world! He tosses our
wrongdoings to the bottom of the sea, never to be dredged
up again. He proceeds to love us extravagantly. Should we
do any less? We should pardon immediately if only out of
gratitude for his grace.

Grace upon Grace

*As you are driving, consider Jesus' grace that casts your
wrongdoing as far as the east is from the west.*

Only by Grace

This righteousness is given through faith in Jesus Christ
to all who believe. There is no difference between Jew and
Gentile, for all have sinned and fall short of the glory of God.

ROMANS 3:22-23 NIV

If church-going Clarissa were honest with herself, she'd
admit that she considered herself better than the woman
at the desk. She'd wrestled with accepting those who were
different. She felt she was purer, smarter, and more socially
acceptable. Basically, Clarissa felt superior. Then the
Sunday sermon brought her up short. *All have sinned*, and
that included her. If the Jews and Gentiles were on equal
footing, then all others were in the same boat as she was.
If there were any redeeming qualities in her life, they came
through the grace of God by faith in Jesus Christ.

The Bible says that all our righteousness is the same as
filthy rags. Our faith in Jesus is what makes us acceptable
to the Father. Next time you're tempted to look down on
someone because of their position or heritage, remember
your condition and where you would be without the gift of
justification through Christ. Then thank the Lord and give
him the glory of your redeemed position.

Grace upon Grace

*Wash dishes and let the cleaning rag serve as a reminder
of how the grace of God redeemed you.*

Peace-Giving Law

Great peace have those who love your law;
nothing can make them stumble.

PSALM 119:165 ESV

When the policeman pulled Tanya over, she couldn't figure
out what she'd done wrong. A sense of worry came over her
about the cost of a ticket. As she rolled down the window,
the officer politely asked her if she knew that her taillight
was broken. He informed her that it is illegal to drive with
a broken taillight. Tanya commented that she was unaware.
The officer said he would give her a warning to get it fixed;
his concern was for her safety. However, the next time she'd
receive a citation.

It is a comfort and a safeguard to know and understand
boundaries. God's law was written for guidance and
protection, not to place burdensome tasks upon us. When
we follow his commands, we're blessed with the peace of his
covering. We know how to act righteously. We know what
sin is and that leads us to obedience. When we hold his law
in high regard and we desire to follow it, we can live life
with security and tranquility.

Grace upon Grace

*Notice fences around homes offering security like you have
through God's saving grace.*

Unforgiveness

Be kind to one another, compassionate, forgiving each
other, just as God in Christ also has forgiven you.

EPHESIANS 4:32 NASB

What Tally had done to Frankie was wrong, but it was
certainly forgivable. However, Frankie wanted to make
Tally sweat it out for a while. After all, she needed to own
what she had done and feel the impact it had on her bestie.
Frankie purposely avoided Tally, making sure she knew she
was being shunned. Then she opened her Bible and was
convicted by the Holy Spirit. Didn't God just forgive her
for something even more damaging? Who was Frankie to
judge and hand out retribution? She corrected her attitude
and called Tally to ask for forgiveness for her unforgiveness.
Life is so sweet within the bounds of righteousness!

We're called to be compassionate and to consider others
before ourselves. How can we do less when we remember
the nails in his body and the blood from his side? All that
Jesus suffered so we can be forgiven should move us to
forgive others quickly, with mercy and grace. Don't hesitate
to absolve those who sin against you. Be moved to act
swiftly out of gratitude for the sacrifice of Jesus on the cross.

Grace upon Grace

*Quickly forgive with mercy and grace the person
who recently wronged you.*

Cleansed by Forgiveness

If we confess our sins, he is faithful and righteous to forgive us our sins and to cleanse us from all unrighteousness.

1 JOHN 1:9 CSB

Lila had acted out of envy and had purposely said things that injured Britta's reputation. Lila had known her comments were lies. But if God would forgive her, couldn't Britta do the same? Lila pondered the question, feeling condemned because she found it impossible to forgive herself. She knew what the Word said about God's cleansing us from our sins, but now the enemy's deception filled her head. Maybe forgiveness wasn't for her. But the Holy Spirit influenced and overpowered her. Soon, she was able to believe the truth. Lila humbled herself and apologized directly to Britta, whom she had harmed.

Sin is vile, and once we succumb to it, we leave ourselves open for the devil's attack. We hesitate to make things right with the Lord and with others. We feel that we can't be forgiven. Scripture promises that if we confess, he will forgive us and wash away our transgressions. As we follow his example to forgive one another, we walk in his righteousness.

Grace upon Grace

Jesus gave you forgiveness, and it is not for you to decide if you are worthy.

Like the Father

"Whenever you stand praying, if you have anything against anyone, forgive him, that your Father in heaven may also forgive you your trespasses."

MARK 11:25 NKJV

As the prayer group filled the room, Candy and Reba stayed on opposite sides avoiding each other. They averted their eyes, not wanting to address the awkward situation. Earlier that day they had argued, and it did not end well. Careless words were spoken, and they left each other in frustration. Now, here they were, wanting to engage in prayer but with obvious dissension between them. When the gathering was opened with Mark 11:25, Candy and Reba approached each other tearfully, then confessed and forgave the harsh words spoken earlier. Confidently, then, they approached the throne of grace.

It's a horrible feeling to be at odds with a friend. It causes us to have awful feelings toward someone we are called to love. It makes us hesitant to pray because we know we have sinned. The Word admonishes us that we are to forgive others so that our Father will forgive us. He hears from heaven when we pray, and he pardons all our sins.

Grace upon Grace

Approach the throne of grace first to address your own sin before you pray.

To Be Unforgiven

"If you don't forgive others,
your Father will not forgive your offenses."

MATTHEW 6:15 CSB

It's difficult to see a loved one suffer at another's hand.
Marsha couldn't bear to see her daughter in such pain,
and she held a grudge against the offender. She envisioned
herself tracking the individual down so she could give
them a piece of her mind. If only the same thing would
happen to them, Marsha thought, giving them a dose of
their own behavior. She stewed, lost sleep, and continued in
unforgiveness, and it kept her from talking to God.

God advises us throughout the Word that if we do not
forgive others, he'll not forgive us. It's such a daunting
thought, to be unforgiven. That alone should drive us to
our knees, but what about the sacrifice of Christ for our
trespasses? Look at the loving lengths God went to so that
we could be forgiven. Out of appreciation alone, we should
forgive others. God knows that pardoning others keeps
us in a right relationship with him. He loves us and wants
us to walk with him, loving and forgiving others as he has
forgiven us.

Grace upon Grace

*Ask God for help if you struggle to forgive someone else,
so you can also be forgiven.*

Countless Sin

Later Peter approached Jesus and said, "How many times do I have to forgive my fellow believer who keeps offending me? Seven times?" Jesus answered, "Not seven times, Peter, but seventy times seven times!"

MATTHEW 18:21-22 TPT

Have you ever known someone who keeps doing the same offensive thing toward you repeatedly? Do you feel weary and tempted to remove yourself from their life, so you don't have to be part of the train wreck? The words "I forgive" stick in your craw with each additional time you must pray them. Is there a number large enough to count the endless times Jesus has pardoned you? There is no number sufficient, yet he promises to continually, without ceasing, forgive when you confess.

The chance that anyone will ever trespass against us four hundred and ninety times is unlikely. However, Jesus expects us to be prepared to forgive countless sin. We are to imitate him and remain aware of how often we must seek his mercy. Don't put a cap on how many times you will offer forgiveness; the grace you have been shown knows no limit.

Grace upon Grace

You can have unlimited messaging on your mobile phone and on your forgiveness.

Identity

Don't let your beauty consist of outward things like
elaborate hairstyles and wearing gold jewelry or
fine clothes, but rather what is inside the heart—the
imperishable quality of a gentle and quiet spirit, which is of
great worth in God's sight.

1 PETER 3:3-4 CSB

The women's Bible study had morphed into a weekly
fashion show. It appeared that the goal was to see who
could outdo the others with the latest designer outfit. The
accessories were over the top with coordinating jewelry,
handbags, and shoes. But there was the one woman, Amina
who didn't seem to care about what she wore. She also
didn't feel uncomfortable as the only one who dressed
casually and often repeated her outfits. Amina knew where
her identity came from. All she cared about was looking
like Jesus inside and out.

We live in a world that is obsessed with image, appearance,
and belongings. Those things don't matter to God; what
matters is the condition of our souls. Sharing a smile and
a kind word is what makes us beautiful. Let's work on the
parts of ourselves that matter most to Jesus.

Grace upon Grace

Look in the mirror and examine the condition of your heart.

Judge Not

"Why do you look at the splinter in your brother's eye
but don't notice the beam in your own eye?"

MATTHEW 7:3 CSB

Have you ever been unpleasantly surprised by someone's
behavior? Maybe you saw them do something and then
brought it up with other people who had seen it too. At
first, you all expressed surprise. You talked about why this
person would act that way and what should be done about
it. You talked about removing the splinter from her eye
without noticing the logs in your own eyes. Everything
anyone ever knew to be true about her was now brought
into question, and you all felt justified because, after all,
none of you would ever do anything like she did.

Oh, how quickly we jump on the follies of other people
without bringing our own issues into question. We judge
and lack compassion, which is exactly the opposite of our
heavenly Father. We bring the gavel down and leave no
room for mercy. We elevate ourselves and believe we are
above such things. Our own downfall is imminent when we
behave this way. Judge not, but instead choose to be filled
with understanding and forgiveness.

Grace upon Grace

*Remove judgment from your lens and replace it with
compassion and understanding.*

Bear With One Another

Bearing with one another, and forgiving each other,
whoever has a complaint against anyone; just as the Lord
forgave you, so must you do also.

COLOSSIANS 3:13 NASB

The quarrel between Olive and Elise was loud and insulting.
Olive believed she was not at fault and Elise was certain
she was. When Olive started to cry, Elise's heart finally
softened. She thought about how she had been accusatory
and realized she lacked compassion. Elise recognized that
maybe Olive's sin wasn't a willful action but rather an error,
one which she should be able to handle. Realizing her own
sin, Elise forgave Olive and sought her forgiveness for her
callous words as well.

Can we be as thoughtful and careful with one another as
we would like others to be with us? God is crystal clear in
Scripture about how we deal with disagreements and how
we must forgive others. When we act as our God requests,
absolving and obliterating any semblance of the wrong in
our hearts and minds, we please him. We start to look more
like his children, emulating the Son.

Grace upon Grace

*Review your motives before you speak,
so that you can show others Jesus.*

Do Not Continue

I acknowledged my sin to you,
and I did not cover my iniquity;
I said, "I will confess my transgressions to the LORD,
and you forgave the iniquity of my sin."

PSALM 32:5 ESV

The doctor's diagnosis made it clear that there were certain foods Tara could no longer eat. She was forced to change her diet or possibly suffer dire consequences. Once she heard the news, Tara was determined to follow her physician's instructions. She knew her body was a temple of the Holy Spirit. To serve God the way she wanted to would require her to be in good health. When she got home, edible pleasures called her name, and she indulged in an unhealthy feast. Afterwards, the reality of her binge drove her back to her knees.

God knows that if we continue in sin, it eventually leads to death. That's why Jesus went to the cross—so we could be forgiven. Jesus' sacrifice allows us to become transformed and to die to sin. Jesus paid the price. If you've not opened your heart to the Savior, won't you ask him to forgive you and bless you with salvation today?

Grace upon Grace

*As someone transformed by the cross,
make necessary changes in how you live.*

Love Your Enemies

"To you who are willing to listen, I say, love your enemies!
Do good to those who hate you."

LUKE 6:27 NLT

You would need to have been living under a rock to miss
the division in our world. Nations against nations, greed
at high levels, and suffering for the common folk. It's no
wonder that people are fearful and wondering if there is any
future at all. It's a heyday for evil yet there is nothing new
under the sun. Evil has existed long before anyone reading
this even lived. It is how we react to evil and to those who
perpetrate it that matters to God.

Jesus said to love our enemies. But how can we do that? It is
difficult to even be around some family members or friends
who don't serve God. When you recall that we're all made in
God's image and he loves us all the same, it gives you pause
when you want to abhor that person. Jesus died for the
world. God loves everyone so much that he allowed his Son
to take the place of all humanity on the cross. Next time you
want to detest someone, remember Jesus' commands, his
sacrifice, and his spoken Word to do good to all.

Grace upon Grace

Pray for someone who feels like your enemy right now.

Undeserved Grace

He has not dealt with us as our sins deserve
or repaid us according to our iniquities.

PSALM 103:10 CSB

Judge Stockton was a stickler that day. He was harsh and demanding to those who had even minor violations. You could feel the tension in the room. People who were waiting to approach the bench kept glancing at each other. As he handed down sentences, gasps filled the room over the exorbitant amount of community time and the huge fees that were imposed. This court was void of any empathy and left everyone feeling as though the burden of their punishment was more than they could bear.

We serve a benevolent heavenly Father who has shown us nothing but mercy for our sins. He doesn't seek retribution but desires to forgive us. The Lord doesn't give us what we deserve for our transgressions. Instead, he gives us what we don't deserve—his grace. When we honor him by respecting who he is, his love overflows onto us. There's no one else who will ever love us more.

Grace upon Grace

Thank God for undeserved grace and freely receive it.

Kindness over Hatred

Hatred stirs up quarrels,
but love makes up for all offenses.

PROVERBS 10:12 NLT

Known around town as the most miserable person alive, people literally crossed the street to avoid Shelly. She never smiled. She was always looking for an altercation. No one tried to befriend her, until one day a young woman moved to town. After hearing the conversations about the hated Shelly, Maribel decided to try loving her. She purposely encountered her and asked her how she was. She told her she loved her, and that Jesus did too. Maribel's persistence won out and eventually the transformation was nothing short of a miracle. Shelly accepted Jesus and her life was changed.

If we can only see beyond the attitude and consider what a person's heart has been through, would we be as kind as Maribel? People need Jesus. Instead of being offended or dismissing someone, we should share the gospel of Jesus Christ. God wants all to come to repentance and we are his messengers. Look beyond the surface, step out, and love others into a recognized need for their Savior, Jesus.

Grace upon Grace

Show kindness to someone who needs to experience the saving grace of Christ.

His Blood

In Him we have redemption through His blood,
the forgiveness of our wrongdoings,
according to the riches of His grace.

EPHESIANS 1:7 NASB

Charlie's accident was almost fatal. When he was transferred to the hospital, the doctors said that without a transfusion he would die. His blood type was pretty rare, so they contacted family members hoping to find that type. A bystander overheard the urgency of their quest and asked the blood type. When he found out his was identical, he graciously offered his own blood. From little hope to great hope, the doctors accepted his offer. They moved quickly, and a life was saved.

We were dead in our sins when Jesus offered his blood on our behalf. Without it, there would be no salvation and no eternal life. It was our blood that should have been drained from our bodies, but God sent his only Son to be broken and bruised on our behalf. We have forgiveness because of his pain and suffering. The punishment was ours, but the perfect and holy Son of God took our place. We have been richly redeemed by the blood of the Lamb.

Grace upon Grace

The blood of the Lamb is so valuable,
giving us forgiveness and redemption.

Be a Peacemaker

"Forgive us our debts,
as we also have forgiven our debtors."

MATTHEW 6:12 CSB

Ursula was hesitant about sharing her past because she was concerned about how she might be received. No one in her church knew that some of her choices had affected some of them. Now Ursula wanted to get right with her relationship with Jesus, and she knew she needed to come clean and ask for forgiveness. She wanted to establish trust with these blessed people. Surprisingly, they all actually knew about her previous sins and had already forgiven her! So blessed was Ursula by their love and support, she grew by leaps and bounds and became one of the greatest servants in her congregation.

So much good comes from being a peacemaker. Withholding mercy only leads to division in the body. We bless others and we honor God when we are tenderhearted toward those who wrong us. When we show swift clemency, we exhibit the heart of God and grow together as his beloved bride. Be quick to silence any hatred and to forgive any offense.

Grace upon Grace

Exhibit loving mercy and grace by being a peacemaker.

Baptism

"Repent and be baptized every one of you in the name of Jesus Christ for the forgiveness of your sins, and you will receive the gift of the Holy Spirit."

ACTS 2:38 ESV

For a long time, Alexandra wanted to become a member of the church. She wanted to align herself with the congregation and all they believed. She studied their tenets and prepared for the ceremony that would give her membership. Once Alexandra was a full-fledged member, she told everyone she could about her church. Her goal was to represent Christ to the best of her ability, and as she did, everyone noticed. Alexandra was soon seen as a valued and dedicated member by the ways in which she served.

When we repent and receive Christ, his Holy Spirit indwells us. At that point we can be baptized. It's a way to publicly say, "I belong to Jesus." By being baptized we outwardly exclaim what we believe in our hearts; that he is our Lord and Savior. As with the woman who joined the church, we are aligning with those who profess a saving grace in Jesus. It's a way to tell everyone that we have confessed, been forgiven, have died to sin, and now live for Christ.

Grace upon Grace

Take the step to be baptized if you haven't been already.

April

He gives grace generously.
As the Scriptures say,
"God opposes the proud
but gives grace to the humble."

JAMES 4:6 NLT

Forgiving Others

"If you forgive other people when they sin against you,
your heavenly Father will also forgive you."

MATTHEW 6:14 NIV

The counselor advised Deirdre that if she would only
forgive and move on, most of her frustration and distress
would dissipate. Living every day with the remembrance
of past conversations was causing her to remain stuck.
Her therapist told her that refusing to forgive was known
to result in health problems in some people, so she was
hurting herself most of all. Deirdre struggled with that
information, still tormented by betrayals and broken trusts.
In the end, she remained in her state of unforgiveness.

Scripture is clear on God's desire for each of us to show
mercy. We are to give clemency to anyone who sins against
us. The Word comes with a warning that if we don't forgive,
we will not be forgiven by God! This is an incredibly
frightful reality. If we hold on to our bitterness, we will most
certainly live a miserable life, emotionally and possibly even
physically. Forgiveness brings freedom for our own souls as
well as for the soul of the one receiving grace.

Grace upon Grace

*Be quick to forgive with mercy and grace;
it will bring freedom to your soul.*

Victory Over Temptation

The temptations in your life are no different from what others experience. And God is faithful. He will not allow the temptation to be more than you can stand. When you are tempted, he will show you a way out so that you can endure.

1 CORINTHIANS 10:13 NLT

It was comforting, helpful, and necessary to hear the advice given by Roma's friend, Piper. Piper confided that she had suffered with a similar temptation. She talked about her experiences both when she gave in to the temptation and when she was victorious. Knowing someone else had fought the same battle was a relief to Roma. Seeing Piper's willingness to share and then walk alongside her was the greatest blessing of hope. It taught Roma that once she won this war, she would be able to help others as well.

We all are tempted; it is our response to that struggle that is important. There is power in Christ to reject sin. If we believe that God will not allow anything too difficult to withstand come our way, we can trust in the victory he will bring. Spending time in God's Word and seeking his guidance aids us in finding a way out.

Grace upon Grace

Stand firm in Christ when temptations arise.

Scriptural Correction

"Be on your guard. If your brother sins, rebuke him,
and if he repents, forgive him."

LUKE 17:3 CSB

We will never be free of sin on this side of heaven. We
have the power in Christ to shut down any desire for
disobedience, yet some believers let their love of pleasure
win the battle. When others fall into trouble, we should
approach them with an attitude of love and understanding.
We are not to mince words, but we are to have a correct and
restorative motive in the delivery. If we are not careful, we
can trespass ourselves. When our corrective measures are
received and there is repentance, we must forgive without
hesitation.

Often when we are doing the Lord's work, the enemy
puts a target on our back. A spiritual victory is frequently
followed by the devil's attack to defeat us and cause us to
sin. We must put on our armor daily as we serve Christ, for
we are delivering blows to Satan's camp. Be on your guard,
know your battle plan, and defeat the steps the enemy takes
against you so that you can be victorious.

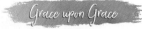

Grace upon Grace

*Seek the Holy Spirit when attempting to correct others
and be aware of your motives.*

Gain Understanding

"Come, let's settle this,"
says the LORD.
"Though your sins are scarlet,
they will be as white as snow."

ISAIAH 1:18 CSB

Mrs. Temple tried to help her student, Timothy, understand the process. They spent study sessions together as Timothy tried to discern the way it all worked. The concept seemed too simple, almost magical, making it hard to believe. If Timothy could only grasp the point, it would open the door to an insight that would alter the rest of his education.

God calls us to gain understanding as it applies to his redemption for us. Many who have had the gospel shared with them say it's just too easy, which conveys they have no understanding of the cross and its purpose. The Lord wants us to know that it is by his power and his love alone that Christ shed his blood on the cross so our scarlet sins can be washed pure white. We owe all our gratitude and praise to the only one who can bring us from death to life.

Grace upon Grace

*Gain a better understanding of the gospel
by getting plugged into a Bible Study.*

Confession

I acknowledged my sin to You,
And I did not hide my guilt;
I said, "I will confess my wrongdoings to the LORD";
And You forgave the guilt of my sin.

PSALM 32:5 NASB

Georgia knew if she only confessed what she had done she would be free of the angst. She was exhausted from the tossing and turning that she had nightly because of her poor choices. It was the shame that held Georgia back. Also, the enemy was taunting that she could never be forgiven and that was a constant theme running through her head. This restrained her longing to move toward the holy one. Knowing her difficulty as only he does, God whispered in Georgia's ear to trust him with her sin, repent, and it would be forgiven and forgotten.

The Lord knows our hearts and he knows when we are truly sorry for our sins. He urges us to come to him, acknowledge our disobedience, and be set free. Due to Jesus' work on the cross, we have open access at any time of the day or night to bring our sins to the Father for cleansing.

Grace upon Grace

*Ask the Lord for forgiveness for the unconfessed sin
you have been holding in your heart.*

Hiding Sin

People who conceal their sins will not prosper, but if they
confess and turn from them, they will receive mercy.

PROVERBS 28:13 NLT

Trent had "borrowed" money from his mother's purse
and then hidden it in his sock drawer. He knew what he
was doing, and even though he had a sinking feeling in
his heart, he also felt entitled. He justified himself—Trent
told himself that he probably deserved it for all the chores
he had done. His mom was always so busy she probably
wouldn't even notice the money missing. When the time
came to use the ill-gotten gain, he just couldn't do it. Trent
went home, told the truth, and gratefully received his
mother's mercy.

It is an awful feeling to conceal something evil in our
hearts. When we willfully sin it eats away at us unless we
have allowed our hearts to harden which is a whole other
danger itself. The only way to live a free and pure life is
to renounce sin and confess any hint of it as quickly as
you realize what you're doing. There is mercy and grace
for those who desire to follow God's commands and live
righteously.

Grace upon Grace

Be mindful of pleasing God not yourself.

Forgiving the Unknowing

While they were nailing Jesus to the cross,
he prayed over and over, "Father, forgive them,
for they don't know what they're doing."

LUKE 23:34 TPT

Although Avery had been the target of River's scorn, she maintained a spirit of loving her. She believed River just didn't know her or understand her. River saw Avery as weird and different, and she chose to ignore her. Avery never held it against her but prayed that one day she would gain entrance into her life and heart. In secret, Avery found ways she could do random acts of kindness for River. She knew this would please her heavenly Father, who she was certain accepted her and cherished her.

The love of Christ that we witness now is the same love that forgave those people who brutally murdered him. It is almost beyond understanding. We believe his sacrifice, we know why he did it, but it is so beyond our understanding. If faced with martyrdom, could we exhibit the same feelings about our torturers? God would certainly provide what we would need in that moment, but it would be entirely his doing and none of ours.

Grace upon Grace

*To be able to forgive like Jesus,
you may need to ask for his help.*

Showing Mercy

To the LORD our God belong mercy and forgiveness,
though we have rebelled against Him.

DANIEL 9:9 NKJV

Abigail amazed those who knew her because she was always willing to forgive without a moment's thought. No matter how much someone trespassed against her, she always gave them grace. Those who shared Abigail's belief in Christ longed to be like her. Those who did not know Jesus felt she needed to stand up for herself. Even so, they admired her composure and kindness. Everyone respected her, for they knew no one else who showed the mercy she did, and, in their hearts, they truly wanted to follow her example.

We all know how our fuses shorten when people continue to do us harm. We want nothing more than to extract them from our lives. Yet we can sin again and again, and our gracious God only shows us mercy. We choose to disobey by going our own way, closing our eyes temporarily so we can enjoy sin for a time. Thankfully, we serve a gracious God who accepts our repentance and restores us to a relationship with him. He never keeps score of our wrongs, and he is always wiping our slate clean.

Grace upon Grace

Renounce sinful desires and live righteously.

Refreshed Through Repentance

Repent, then, and turn to God, so that your sins may be wiped out, that times of refreshing may come from the Lord.

ACTS 3:19 NIV

The tears fell in torrents as Rhona repented to Kara of her behavior, Rhona had sinned against Kara, and the shame brought a color to her face, revealing a deep disappointment in herself. At least Rhona would be free of the overwhelming guilt, but she actually believed the relationship would never be repaired. Then Kara lifted her chin and spoke words that felt like balm to her broken heart. Kara completely forgave Rhona with mercy and love. With this full forgiveness came a chance to be free from any reminder of her sin ever again.

Don't you see Jesus in this story? He beckons us to bring our debts to him; he has already paid the price. He longs to forgive us and set us back on the road to a right relationship with him. He supplies us with peace and restoration to walk in unlimited goodness and mercy with him throughout our lives. He gave everything to have us and the desires that we have to be free of the sin that besets us.

Grace upon Grace

Wipe a dirty window or mirror, and note it is that easy for you to confess and be forgiven.

New Covenant

"This is my blood of the covenant, which is poured out
for many for the forgiveness of sins."

MATTHEW 26:28 ESV

The room was filled with the disciples sitting at a table
partaking of the Passover meal with their Lord. They may
have talked about the excitement of recent healings and
the wisdom of his Words as he taught the masses. Little did
they know that his sharing of the wine and the bread was
pointing to a coming event. When Jesus offered the bread,
he used it as symbolism to represent his broken body; the
wine is to identify his blood. These two symbols represent
his death on a cross.

The old covenant between God and Abraham was sealed by
the circumcision of all boys on their eighth day of life. The
new covenant was sealed by the spilling of blood at Christ's
crucifixion. When Jesus took the first communion in the
upper room with his disciples, he shared the bread and
wine as a symbol of his sacrifice which was poured out and
shattered on our behalf for the forgiveness of sins. We take
it today in memory of this sacrifice.

Grace upon Grace

*Look at a picture of the Last Supper with gratitude
for the new covenant.*

Broken Bread

I pass on to you what I received from the Lord himself. On the night when he was betrayed, the Lord Jesus took some bread and gave thanks to God for it. Then he broke it in pieces and said, "This is my body, which is given for you. Do this in remembrance of me."

1 Corinthians 11:23-24 NLT

Every night after dinner, Denton, as head of the family, would take out his Bible. He went verse by verse through the Scriptures teaching his family. He knew that the best way to know God was by seeking him through dedicated time in the Word. Denton told his family how the Holy Spirit had led him over the years. He spoke of God's continued faithfulness. One night a week the whole family would have communion. Denton taught the importance of taking it with discernment and to scrutinize their own hearts.

When Jesus requests something of us, it must be met solemnly and sincerely. Remembering his appeal to receive the bread and wine which represent his crucifixion must be taken seriously. Scripture tells us to examine ourselves to see if we understand Christ's sacrifice.

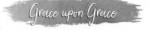

Grace upon Grace

Have communion at home and seriously consider all that it represents.

Forgive as He Does

"I will forgive their wickedness
and will remember their sins no more."

HEBREWS 8:12 NIV

Disappointed as they were, Phillip's parents decided it
was more important to show grace to their child than to
openly express their displeasure. There were consequences
to Phillip's actions, but it was the better path to present
love and forgiveness instead of anger. Their desire was to
emulate the way God had forgiven them over the years,
delivering a lesson of his mercy for all who repent. The
preteen accepted the forgiveness with humility, fully
owning his wrongdoing and receiving the appropriate
discipline. Phillip knew from his parents' handling of the
situation that without the shadow of a doubt, he was loved.
He knew the subject would never be revisited because his
parents acted as God would have acted.

We should all forgive and forget as the Lord does regardless
of the situation. If the Creator of the universe responds with
this kind of grace, he can empower us to do the same. Be
holy as he is holy, forgiving and loving in the name of Jesus.

Grace upon Grace

*Ask God for grace and wisdom to
offer forgiveness in difficult situations.*

Golgotha

When they came to the place called The Skull,
there they crucified Him and the criminals,
one on the right and the other on the left.

LUKE 23:33 NASB

Daren was accused along with the others, but he was an innocent bystander. He was, nevertheless, charged the same as they were and placed in a cell alongside them. There they sat until their fates were decided. The day came for the criminals to receive their sentencing, and although Daren knew he himself wasn't guilty, there was nothing he could do so he kept silent. There was no alibi and the evidence pointed to him as much as to the others. The fact that Daren was in the wrong place at the wrong time brought sentencing that was swift and heavy.

Jesus never sinned yet was broken on the cross for the sins of the world. He shared his place of punishment on Golgotha with two men who deserved to be penalized. The one who believed him to be the Messiah asked that he remember him when he came into his kingdom. As Jesus bled and died, he promised the repentant man that he would be in paradise with him that very day.

Grace upon Grace

*Thank Jesus for taking your place and paying
for your sin on the cross.*

Sea of Sin

He will again have compassion on us;
he will tread our iniquities underfoot.
You will cast all our sins into the depths of the sea.

MICAH 7:19 ESV

As the judge was about to hand down the verdict and require the fine, a stranger stepped forward. He listened as the announcement came that there would be a one thousand dollar fine. Rupert crumbled because he knew he had no means to pay. The compassionate stranger stepped forward and took out his checkbook. He approached the bench and said, "I will pay the fine for this man." The judge was stunned but allowed the kindness. Rupert wept, struggling to understand why someone would care for him in this way.

When we think of all that God has forgiven us and the kindness he has shown by not casting us into hell for our sins, we should weep with gratitude. We did not pay the penalty for our sin; Jesus paid it for us. He stomped out our trespasses and when we confess, he drowns them at the bottom of the sea. We don't deserve his grace, yet it is given to us in abundance.

Grace upon Grace

Sing a song of praise for the grace you don't deserve.

Attitude like Stephen

Then he fell on his knees and cried out, "Lord, do not hold this sin against them." When he had said this, he fell asleep.

ACTS 7:60 NIV

The falsehoods aimed in Hannah's direction moved her to truthfully address them. She had no idea that their hurtful actions were perpetrated because they felt threatened by her. The knowledge and the authority with which she spoke made them envious. The favor she received due to her wisdom and anointing caused them to plot against her. Once aware, she continued as always, for she was called by God to speak on his behalf.

When jealous men revolted against Stephen instead of staying quiet, he gave them a tour through the Old Testament to the crucifixion. Unable to see the wisdom of his words, they plotted to take him down permanently. He didn't waver. As they wrongfully stoned him, he prayed that God would not hold their sin against them. May we have the same humble attitude as Stephen did staying true to Jesus regardless of the cost.

Grace upon Grace

Pray for those who hurt you or speak against you.

Most Extravagant Grace

"I—yes, I alone—will blot out your sins for my own sake
and will never think of them again."

ISAIAH 43:25 NLT

As leader, Iona called them all to a high standard. He
insisted on modesty, responsibility, and humility. She taught
the young group of women to infuse these traits into their
daily lives. They were new Christians, yet ambassadors
for Jesus regardless. Because they claimed Christ as their
Savior, they also carried his reputation to the world. When
the news reached Iona that the women had poorly chosen
one evening to have a night on the town, she knew she
must forgive them. Because the evening had turned a bit
wild, she needed to encourage them to confess their sin,
receive God's forgiveness, and believe they could start over
with a clean slate.

God's holy and righteous character results in his enormous
compassion. It is who he is, and he never changes. He
reveals himself as the greatest love there ever was. To
demonstrate his goodness, he forgives and forgets. We who
are in Christ are the recipients of the most extravagant
grace in existence.

Grace upon Grace

Give someone an extravagant gift of grace.

Show Mercy

"Blessed are the merciful, for they will receive mercy."

MATTHEW 5:7 NASB

Belle neglected to show any amount of leniency to her offender, Sebastian. Any advance to make amends was ignored as Belle continued to nurse her anger. Sebastian wrote a note of apology, but Belle would not accept it. He left a gift of goodwill on her doorstep but that, too, was rejected. A mutual friend pled Sebastian's case, but no charity was shown by Belle. Then one day Belle said something hurtful. When she tried to atone for her thoughtless words, she got no mercy. Suddenly, she understood her own hardened heart.

We are promised the blessing of mercy if we are merciful to others. If we refuse to offer grace, we will find it unavailable to us as well. God never withholds any good thing from those whose walk is blameless. He is generous and benevolent. As Christ followers, we must act the same.

Grace upon Grace

Quickly dispense mercy to all who ask for it.

Pray for the Sick

Is anyone among you sick? Let him call for the elders of the church, and let them pray over him, anointing him with oil in the name of the Lord.

JAMES 5:14 ESV

The team at the hospital had exhausted every medical treatment possible, yet Trina's suffering continued. She was wasting away before her family's eyes, and the pain of watching it was unbearable. They believed, but their faith wavered when they prayed for healing. When they reached the point of desperation, they called the church and a group of prayer warriors rushed to their side. God worked a miracle and answered with healing. The lives of those who witnessed it were changed from that point on.

Why do we hesitate when Scripture clearly says to call the elders and let them pray and anoint with oil? Is it because we don't believe healing is for today? God may not grant healing on this earth. He may, instead, take his precious one home. Nevertheless, we are given instructions in his Word, and we should follow them in faith, trusting that if it is his will a miracle of healing will happen.

Grace upon Grace

Pray for healing over someone who is sick.

Our Story

He was wounded for our transgressions,
He was bruised for our iniquities;
The chastisement for our peace was upon Him,
And by His stripes we are healed.

ISAIAH 53:5 NKJV

Drew intervened when the old woman was mugged, and
he was horribly beaten in the process. His heroic actions
were met with a battering by a baseball bat, but it gave the
woman, Daisy, time to escape. The police apprehended
the offender, and Drew was applauded for his bravery.
He learned that Daisy had been admitted to the hospital
anyway. Because of Daisy's health issues she would have
died if he had not intervened.

This is like our story. If Jesus had not stepped in to take
our place on the cross, we would have suffered eternal
separation from God in hell. He endured torture knowing
that there was no other way we could be reconciled to God.
Without his sacrifice, we would be stuck in the sickness of
our sin and destined to live without salvation or our Savior.
Live your life well for Jesus, knowing that without his loving
atonement, you would be lost.

Grace upon Grace

If you have surrendered your life to God's will, then live well.

God's Grace

You are saved by grace through faith,
and this is not from yourselves; it is God's gift.

EPHESIANS 2:8 CSB

When Dorie's car broke down, she had no idea where she would find the money to repair it. And as a single mom without a car, she wouldn't be able to get to work or to take her children to school. This would lead to so many difficulties and hardships. Dorie did the only thing she knew to do—she prayed. God was faithful; he gave the idea to a distant friend who was unaware of her need to anonymously send her some money. It was all Dorie needed, and the exact amount of the repair.

We've been freely given the greatest gift with salvation through the death and resurrection of Christ. We did nothing to deserve it. In fact, our sin should have destined us to destruction. In his mercy and grace, God not only saved us, but he also gave us the power to believe. We would never have come to the realization that we needed a Savior without the prompting of the Holy Spirit. Doesn't it amaze you and make you grateful beyond words?

Grace upon Grace

Anonymously send money to someone who needs it.

Without Sin

As they continued to ask him, he stood up and said to them, "Let him who is without sin among you be the first to throw a stone at her."

JOHN 8:7 ESV

Abby and Nadia were raking their friend, Temple, over the coals for her attempt to shoplift. A sales associate saw everything, including Temple handling the item, beginning to put it in her purse, but then putting it back. As she looked at the other girls, she noticed that both Abby and Nadia had been in the store earlier doing the same thing. She talked to them all, telling them that she knew what they had done. Abby and Nadia shouldn't be judging Temple so quickly when they had acted in the same manner.

Jesus knows we are all sinners. He knows that on this side of heaven we will continue to be tempted. Sadly, sometimes we will cave to our sinful desires. He knows our propensity to view other's actions harsher than we view our own, so he made it clear that we are not to judge. Don't go looking for others' faults. Look closely at yourself and check your own motives. If there is sin, confess it and get right with God.

Grace upon Grace

Stop criticizing others and overlooking your own sinfulness.

Because of Him

I am writing to you, little children, because your sins have
been forgiven you on account of His name.

1 JOHN 2:12 NASB

There was a celebration planned for Mrs. Horne's class, not
that they deserved it. All the children had been particularly
unruly that week. Mrs. Horne was being named instructor
of the year so the class would be on stage with her at the
award ceremony. There would be cake and ice cream
afterwards so the much-loved teacher could party with
her class. The event was planned and publicized already so
there was no canceling it. Mrs. Horne showed a lot of mercy
and allowed the kids to be involved as her accomplishments
were being recognized.

At Christ's resurrection when forgiveness was offered
through the blood of Jesus, we were shown the most
extravagant grace. Our sin nature was still intact and
nothing we did could alter that. By his powerful, almighty
name, God created a way for us to be saved; we must give
him all the glory. We are blessed beyond measure, forgiven,
and made righteous. We are the recipients of eternal life
because of his nature and great name.

Grace upon Grace

Praise his almighty, beautiful name
and give him your whole heart.

Awe and Adoration

With you there is forgiveness,
so that you may be revered.

PSALM 130:4 CSB

The owner of the company, Mr. Galton, had rightfully gained deep respect from his employees. He always acted in the best interest of the company and of his workers. If someone made an error, he didn't berate them. Privately, he would explain their mistake and how they could do it differently the next time. Not only was Mr. Galton admired, but he was also loved. This inspired his staff to do their best to please him.

Our gratitude for God's grace for us by the forgiveness of our sins should garner the greatest obedience and reverence. If we had been left with no way of redemption, we would be the most desperate and lost humanity. We would be destined for eternal destruction, but because of his goodness we are offered salvation and eternity with him. We should be shouting his love and the news of the path to salvation from the rooftops. He deserves our entire devotion and complete submission as we view him with awe and adoration.

Grace upon Grace

Believe and receive all that God's grace has done for you.

Identifying with Jesus

What are you waiting for? Get up and be baptized. Have your sins washed away by calling on the name of the Lord.

ACTS 22:16 NLT

Ellen Sparks, a business owner, wanted so badly to close the private deal of a lifetime, but the client was dragging his feet. She encouraged and influenced him by reiterating all the benefits he would have by going forward with the purchase. Elvin Dorn continued to hesitate though, and Ellen started to wonder if she should put the business back on the market. When she told Mr. Dorn that it was possible that he would soon lose the opportunity to purchase her company, he became suddenly inspired and moved to seal the acquisition with some urgency.

Identifying with Jesus' death and resurrection should be a no-brainer, yet many treat baptism like it doesn't matter. Anyone who has gone under the water to signify their forgiveness from sin and as an expression of their new birth in Christ will tell you it's an important step to take in faith. Don't hesitate to align yourself with the body of Christ in order to show your faith in Jesus to all.

Grace upon Grace

Through you, others will hear of the love and forgiveness of Christ.

Accepting the Consequences

Against You, You only, I have sinned
And done what is evil in Your sight,
So that You are justified when You speak
And blameless when You judge.

PSALM 51:4 NASB

Helen was afraid to go to her husband, Thomas, and admit what she had done. He would be perfectly within his rights to be angry with her carelessness and lack of respect for their financial well-being. Helen had always struggled with impulse buying but this purchase was the most extravagant yet. Thomas had warned her time and again that she had to be wary of her expenditures. In humility, she went to him and apologized, agreeing to discuss any major purchases with him until she could learn to get a handle on her spending.

Sometimes our shame makes us hesitant to go to God and confess. David is our example, for he went in humility to his Lord, acknowledging his wrongdoing and taking responsibility for how vile his sin truly was. He accepted the consequences with humility and grace. We should respect God but not fear his correction, for it comes from his loving hand.

Grace upon Grace

Stay in a right relationship with the Lord through correction, confession, and forgiveness.

All Should Repent

Truly, these times of ignorance God overlooked,
but now commands all men everywhere to repent.

ACTS 17:30 NKJV

Molly had made an idol of her appearance. She obsessed about being in perfect shape and spent hours in the gym. She bought only the most fashionable clothes and the best, high-end cosmetics. Molly committed her earnings to surgical procedures that would keep her looking young. This soon put her in a precarious financial position. She forced herself to cut up her credit cards and make payment plans with her creditors. By necessity, Molly then put herself on a strict budget.

At one time man created idols out of gold. Remember the Israelites and the golden calf? Today's verse refers to a period when God overlooked man's ignorance. However, a time came when a new commandment was set in place that all should repent and acknowledge him as the one true God. We cannot create our own deity. There is only one Lord and Savior. Without recognizing his preeminence and receiving his salvation, we are lost. Repenting and receiving his forgiveness for our sins will set us on the path to righteousness and eternity with him.

Grace upon Grace

Recognize what has become an idol in your life.

Appeasement for Sin

He is the propitiation for our sins, and not for ours only but also for the sins of the whole world.

1 JOHN 2:2 ESV

The manager, Denise, was the only one who could offer appeasement for her company's gross error. She alone was trusted by her boss, Mr. Trenton, to make things right. Her co-workers had made decisions without her involvement. They had changed the agreements without approval and believed they were making things better for everyone. This, unfortunately, put the company into a position to be threatened with a lawsuit. Since Denise was not involved in the scheme, her reputation was intact, and her word would be honored. She was the only hope of a resolution.

If Jesus had not made amends for all sin with his broken body and shed blood, we would be left without any lifeline. There would be no redemption for he alone was able to atone for all of our transgressions. Our existence here and in eternity depends solely on the cross. Our acceptance of the glorious gift freely given to us by God is our choice to accept or reject through freewill. We need to realize that there is no other way.

Grace upon Grace

*Go to Jesus—the only way for you
to get atonement for your sin.*

Right vs Evil

Never repay evil for evil to anyone.
Respect what is right in the sight of all people.

ROMANS 12:17 NASB

Lena's blood was boiling at the attack lodged against her. She was truthfully in shock that anyone could come up with such a mean-spirited act. Her temptation was to concoct a similarly angry response with a bit more kick. But she knew better, and she knew what God desired of her, so she would let this go. God would take care of the whole issue because vengeance is his and his alone. Lena would stay in the Lord's good graces and simply pray, asking that he give her the power in her heart to forgive and to trust him to bring the truth to light.

We're never to act in an evil way toward another either maliciously or accidentally. There should be no avenue for any type of ill will because we have instruction in God's Word telling us to love one another and to consider others ahead of ourselves. If we have the fruit of the Spirit, we should quickly move from anger to forgiveness. We are instructed to act righteously toward one another. We are to be holy as God is holy.

Grace upon Grace

*Act with compassion and righteousness
even when others cause you harm.*

Soft Answer

A gentle answer turns away anger,
but a hard word stirs up wrath.

PROVERBS 15:1 CSB

Randi continued to raise her voice, but her husband stayed calm. The fact that he wouldn't meet her volume began to influence her. Suddenly Randi felt ashamed and began to settle down. She knew she needed to listen to her husband's side of things and not become so enraged. Once she composed herself, she understood the situation and began to feel compassion instead of anger. The couple continued the discussion with love and respect and found themselves laughing at the silly argument later that day.

Scripture is clear about how we are to react in a tense situation. We are to speak with understanding and encouragement. We are to consider the other person before we think of ourselves. That means that we control our tempers and listen to the other side of the story. We pray for wisdom and discernment so that we have insight from the Holy Spirit into others' struggles and how best to minister to them. Start by learning through the power of the Spirit about how to set aside any rage and to speak the truth in love.

Grace upon Grace

Exercise self-control by having a soft answer for others.

Maturing in Christ

Get rid of all bitterness, rage, anger, harsh words, and
slander, as well as all types of evil behavior.

EPHESIANS 4:31 NLT

Randolph was definitively cantankerous. His family could
have only short visits with him before he insulted and
angered them. He knew the truth about Jesus and had
even asked him for forgiveness in a tender moment, but it
ended there. Randolph never prayed, never read the Word,
and never followed any spiritual disciplines. This left him
subject to his sin nature. This raged on in his character
because he wasn't seeking maturity in Christ nor any help
from the Holy Spirit.

The Bible is complete with all the instructions we need to
live a life filled with the fruit of the Spirit. There's no reason
to give into sinful behavior because we have evidence of
what God does with a willing and surrendered heart. It is
our responsibility to answer any temptation from the evil
one with the truth of God's Word. It is our choice whether
we'll studiously prepare ourselves to react as Jesus would or
succumb to evil.

Grace upon Grace

Live your life so others see Christ in you.

May

The grace of God has appeared that
offers salvation to all people.

TITUS 2:11 NIV

He Will Equip

Mary said, "My soul magnifies the Lord,
and my spirit rejoices in God my Savior."

LUKE 1:46-47 ESV

Rae had been chosen and would answer the need to
minister to those in a foreign land. The assignment was way
beyond her ability and her comfort zone. She decided that
instead of allowing fear to enter her heart, she would begin
to praise God joyfully. Through faith, God would equip Rae
to accomplish all that was necessary to take each step.

When the angel came to Mary and announced that God
had picked her to birth his one and only Son, he found a
willing participant. She was curious yet still humble with
her response. She certainly had some questions for she
had not known a man, but she also had strong faith. The
angel explained that the Holy Spirit would come upon her,
and then she would be with child. She glorified God and
magnified his holy name with this amazing news. Will you
be ready and eager to answer God's call for your life?

Grace upon Grace

*Try to have a heart and faith like Mary
for whatever God asks of you.*

Set Free

> "Through Jesus the forgiveness of sins is proclaimed to you. Through him everyone who believes is set free from every sin, a justification you were not able to obtain under the law of Moses."
>
> ACTS 13:38-39 NIV

The little town was failing under the leadership of a power-hungry mayor. Fines for ridiculous things were levied against the members of the community just so he could put more money in his own pockets. Those who committed actual crimes were excused on technicalities, so he could enlist them to do his undercover dirty work. When it came time for re-election, a new candidate entered the scene. This man was righteous. He had the best interests of the people in mind. They were liberated from the evil politician and thrived under the leadership of a good and honorable man.

Without our Savior, evil would continue to reign. We would definitely be enslaved to it. Jesus came to earth to pay our debt, forgive our sin, and offer a transformed life to all who believe in his name. If we confess our trespasses, he will justify us through the washing of his blood. His great sacrifice set us free.

Grace upon Grace

Thank Jesus for setting you free from the law of sin and death.

Loving Your Neighbor

If you really fulfill the royal law according to the Scripture,
"You shall love your neighbor as yourself," you do well.

JAMES 2:8 NKJV

Cora and her husband, Devin, had always talked about
getting together with their neighbors, but it was just that—
talk. They could never seem to make the time to invite them
for dinner or even spend a few minutes chatting about the
weather. Now that Devin had passed, Cora really needed
more than a meal or a casual conversation. She needed
friends who would come alongside her in her sorrow.
If only the couple had nurtured those neighborhood
relationships, they might have had a closeness that would
feed her soul in this time of need.

How can we say we love our neighbors when we live next
door year after year and don't even know their names? We
are too busy, and many are desperately lonely. Whether we
take a plate of cookies or send an invitation for a visit, think
about how you can show a nearby resident love today.

Grace upon Grace

*Reach out and share the love of Christ
with someone in your community.*

Never Perish

"God loved the world in this way: He gave his one and only Son, so that everyone who believes in him will not perish but have eternal life. For God did not send his Son into the world to condemn the world, but to save the world through him."

JOHN 3:16-17 CSB

The movie portrayed a fantasyland where all injuries were immediately healed, death did not exist, and everyone had a fulfilling life of never-ending joy. As the audience watched you could see they were mesmerized by the beauty of a world where there were no problems. When it was revealed at the end that it was a hoax played on unsuspecting citizens by an evil government, the audience was horrified. The lights came on at the end, and everyone was very glad it was only a motion picture.

When judgment day comes it will not be a ruse, and the facts about heaven and hell will be eternally real. We can act now and receive God's gift of his only Son as our Savior. His death on the cross provided our salvation. His is the only name that can save. The last thing God wants is for anyone to be lost, for he desires that all will come to repentance.

Grace upon Grace

*Make sure you aren't just acting
but are fully surrendering your life to Jesus.*

Bearing Your Heart

"Tear your heart and not merely your garments."
Now return to the LORD your God,
For He is gracious and compassionate,
Slow to anger, abounding in mercy
And relenting of catastrophe.

JOEL 2:13 NASB

Holly knew what she had done was naughty. Her parents
asked her to apologize, but she wouldn't do it. Inside, she
was embarrassed and couldn't look at her friend, Emily,
let alone speak to her. Holly's parents saw it as defiance,
so rightfully, they sent her to her room. She cried until
they chose to show her grace. This softened her heart, and
Holly's feelings of shame became safe with those she had
disobeyed. This allowed her to bare her heart, repent, and
then say she was sorry to Emily.

All it took was the parents' compassion to help little Holly
confide and confess. Feelings of guilt can cause us to pull
inside ourselves, making communication difficult. We
know our God is kind and full of grace for us. We can take
our darkest sins to the Lord, and he will forgive us.

Grace upon Grace

Allow God's compassion and grace
to help you lay your sin before him.

A Heavenly Kingdom

He has rescued us from the kingdom of darkness and
transferred us into the Kingdom of his dear Son, who
purchased our freedom and forgave our sins.

COLOSSIANS 1:13-14 NLT

The young prince was held in the dungeon as the imposter
assumed his throne. The young royal had been away
fighting a war for years and had grown into a man. The liar,
who claimed to be him, had fooled everyone by arriving
back the day before the true prince. He knew all he needed
to assume the prince's life, sharing his secrets as evidence. A
trusted old courier who knew the prince as a child, testified
about his true identity. The rightful man was restored to the
throne, and the fraud was imprisoned.

There is only one way of salvation and that is through Jesus
Christ. False prophets will claim to be him, but his chosen
ones recognize him as the Savior of the world. He paid
the price for those the Father has given to him, and he is
making them royalty by the shedding of his blood. Now all
who know him look forward to a heavenly kingdom where
they will reign forever with the true King of kings and Lord
of lords.

Grace upon Grace

Be aware of false prophets, so you can recognize the true king.

Good For Evil

Do not repay evil with evil or insult with insult. On the
contrary, repay evil with blessing, because to this you were
called so that you may inherit a blessing.

1 PETER 3:9 NIV

When Serenity loudly berated another teen girl, a crowd
gathered to listen. They all waited for Taran to respond
with some choice words of her own. Instead, Taran
complimented the nasty girl. No one understood, especially
Serenity, who received kindness to her own nastiness.
When she retorted with meanness again instead of ending
the diatribe, the other kids shook their heads and walked
off with Taran. Serenity was left standing alone with all her
evil intentions.

God calls us to do good when we are harmed. We are never
to seek vengeance. We are to remain peaceful, knowing that
our God is the one who judges. It may not happen today,
but the day will come when all evil will be seen for what it
is. Then it will be too late for those who never decided to
follow Jesus. If someone hurts you, bless them. When they
see your good works, it may be the very thing that leads
them to faith in Christ.

Grace upon Grace

*Turn the other cheek and show Jesus' love
to someone who hurts you.*

Good Fruit

As those who have been chosen of God, holy and beloved,
put on a heart of compassion, kindness, humility,
gentleness, and patience; bearing with one another, and
forgiving each other, whoever has a complaint against
anyone; just as the Lord forgave you, so must you do also.

COLOSSIANS 3:12-13 NASB

The library staff all remembered when the boss woman,
Phyllis, would be most unpleasant. Something had
happened, though, and now she was very different. She
greeted them each morning with a smile, and she asked
sincerely how they were doing. Phyllis now gently informed
the staff in sharp contrast to her old ways of yelling orders.
If mistakes were made, she didn't embarrass anyone
publicly. When someone got the nerve up to ask what
happened to her, she only needed one word—Jesus.

Christ makes all the difference. Without him we are
miserable creatures left to our own evil desires. With
Jesus, we start to exhibit gentleness, patience, humility,
forgiveness, compassion, and kindness. As we show the
fruit of the Spirit to the world, people see the difference in
us, and they want what we have.

Grace upon Grace

Consider that you were chosen to bear good fruit.

Forgiveness Brings Freedom

How joyful is the one
whose transgression is forgiven,
whose sin is covered!

PSALM 32:1 CSB

Mason held grudges and berated people in the church. He even gossiped about those who offended him. Some of the elders approached him and told him this behavior was not pleasing to God. He was to forgive as he had been forgiven. Mason became offended and called other people in the church to complain about those who he claimed had wrongfully judged him. Eventually as he continued to harbor his sin, Mason became very sick. It didn't stop him from badmouthing the people who tried to help him.

Medical professionals claim that unforgiveness and bitterness can make us very unhealthy. The Lord loves us and wants us to live a free and blessed life in Christ. He knows forgiveness brings freedom. The burden of blaming others without offering absolution places us in the position to be unforgiven by God. Seek to forgive quickly and you'll experience the benefit of peace and God's blessings over your life.

Grace upon Grace

Forgive as you have been forgiven and live in freedom.

No Record

Lord, if you kept an account of iniquities,
Lord, who could stand?

PSALM 130:3 CSB

There was a point system in the office meant to encourage
and motivate the employees. Each month, a ranking was
released which showed the top producer down to the staff
member who had the furthest to go. The chart was color
coded with the top entries in a cheery yellow and the least
successful in a drab gray. The boss thought this was a
proactive way to get people to hustle, but for those at the
bottom of the list, it felt like a permanent mark on their
record.

If there was no forgiveness and every sin was memorialized,
we would be doomed. Our just God would have to
condemn us. The world would be headed for hell if not for
the sacrifice of Jesus, who paid all our debts on the cross.
Thank God for his grace and the fact that he doesn't hold
our sins against us. Be grateful for the grace that, upon our
confession, casts the sins of the repentant into the depths of
the sea.

Grace upon Grace

*Express your gratitude to Jesus for his grace
that keeps no record of wrong.*

Check Your Motives

If another believer is overcome by some sin, you who are
godly should gently and humbly help that person back
onto the right path. And be careful not to fall into the same
temptation yourself.

GALATIANS 6:1 NLT

Sheila belonged to the prayer group, and she asked for
intercession for herself and for Patricia, the woman she was
going to approach. Sheila was anxious that Patricia would
not receive correction very well even though Sheila would
be using Scripture. She knew the others had not been very
successful when approaching this prickly person so why
would she be different? She started to lose her nerve, but
then someone offered Galatians 6:1 as their verse for the
evening. As she approached Patricia, she could see that all
the prayers were answered. She marveled as the difficult
woman reflected grace and humility.

It's our duty to correct and rescue a sister or brother from
spiritual harm. As we do that, we're to guard ourselves so
we do not suffer the same temptation. We must be right
with God so we can go in humility and the power of the
Holy Spirit.

Grace upon Grace

*Check your motives before correcting others
and be moved by love.*

Those in Distress

"Should you not also have had compassion on your fellow
servant, just as I had pity on you?"

MATTHEW 18:33 NKJV

It was as if a load of bricks fell off Amber's shoulders when
her friend, Ernestina said there was no need to pay her
back. She was blessed by the generosity of her long-time
buddy and said she would always remember the kindness.
As Amber went on her way, she passed a young woman
on the street with a sign asking for money to buy food for
her children. Thinking she was able-bodied and could be
working to pay for her own necessities, Amber, who had
been forgiven her debt, walked right past the needy mother.
Obviously, the compassion Amber had been shown by
Ernestina was lost on her.

God expects us to show tenderness to others. If we have
been on the receiving end of benevolence, we should be even
more eager to show charity to those in need. When we judge
someone instead, we bring judgment upon ourselves. We
should always treat people as we would want to be treated.
We should always offer aid in a time of poverty. We need to
be the hands and feet of Jesus to those who are in distress.

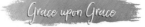

Grace upon Grace

*Joyfully provide for someone out of the blessings
you have been given.*

Unbearable

My guilty deeds have gone over my head;
Like a heavy burden they weigh too much for me.

PSALM 38:4 NASB

Elsie had been sullen and distant for days. Her parents chalked it up to being sixteen and decided to give her some space. The girl began to skip meals, saying she didn't feel well and spending hours alone. Mom and Dad noticed Elsie's countenance as it grew darker, and finally felt it was time to step in. Elsie admitted that she had made some poor choices that had caused her friends to oust her from their group. Overwhelmed by the emotions and the shame, she confessed to her parents, and thereby started taking the first step toward healing.

We all know the feelings of sorrow when we choose to go our own way. A single sin left unchecked leads to another, and soon the weight is more than we can bear. Praise Jesus that he made a way for us to confess our heavy burdens and give us forgiveness for our transgressions. We get to start with a fresh slate. What a glorious thought, that we are set free by repentance and the blood of the Lamb!

Grace upon Grace

*Don't hesitate to confess your sins
and be free of the burden of guilt.*

Silently Praying

Whoever belittles his neighbor lacks sense,
but a man of understanding remains silent.

PROVERBS 11:12 ESV

Mike was watering his lawn as he overheard one neighbor, Luke, raising his voice to another, Emory. It was over a property line and involved a fallen tree. Mike was shocked as the conversation went from a physical disagreement to a personal belittling. Luke and Emory cast insults back and forth, and they nearly came to blows. Mike, who was tending his garden, could have intervened but it wouldn't have been received well. Instead, he prayed for his neighbors that they would see their sin, confess, and work together for the good of both of their properties.

We should never speak poorly of someone to their faces or behind their backs. We are to think about things that are lovely. We are called to encourage one another. As we love like Jesus commanded us to do, we will naturally want to be helpful and to serve our fellow man. We must be led by Holy Spirit to ever intervene; otherwise, we do well to stay silent and pray. Commit to doing good things by asking God to intervene in the hearts and minds of those who are unwise.

Grace upon Grace

Hold your tongue and pray when you see foolishness acted out.

Unending Love

"My soul glorifies the Lord
and my spirit rejoices in God my Savior."

LUKE 1:46-47 NIV

It was as if the skies were opened for the first time. The evening was adorned by the glowing sun and sweetened by the music of the birds. Andrea had fallen in love and knew that this young man, Brandon, was the one. She had never felt this way before; she was so certain, so at peace with their decision which would affect everything in their lives going forward. Andrea and Brandon spoke of marriage and children, and she knew a proposal was imminent. Her joy knew no bounds.

If we truly understand and believe all that God feels about us and has done for us, we should be the happiest of all. Our joy should overflow, knowing that our lives and our eternity are secure in Christ. We serve a God who continuously blesses us with his presence and invites us to come before his throne. He never takes his eyes off of us, and he loves us unendingly and unconditionally. We are above all blessed, and our faces should show it. Praise his great and holy name!

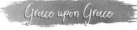
Grace upon Grace

Let yourself be overwhelmed at the thought of spending eternity in paradise with God.

The Same Mouth

Blessing and cursing come pouring out of the same mouth.
Surely, my brothers and sisters, this is not right!

JAMES 3:10 NLT

The way Laken would comment on someone else's strengths
and then viciously blast their inadequacies made her look
like she had a split personality. How could someone speak
such goodness and then follow it with such evil? It made
the people around her uncomfortable, and it certainly
caused them to keep their distance. This only fueled
Laken's fire. Finally, someone prayed and fasted; then they
approached Laken to discuss her hurtful words.

Gossip and foul language should never leave a Christian's
mouth. We will give account for every careless word.
Remembering God is always listening, we need to keep
watch over our conversations and be alert to confess
immediately when we sin.

Grace upon Grace

Make your words a blessing and encouragement to others.

Droning On

When there are many words, sin is unavoidable,
but the one who controls his lips is prudent.

PROVERBS 10:19 CSB

The man in the corner practically fell off his chair as he
drifted off during the long speech. It was meant to be a
small gathering where everyone would have the chance to
speak but one person, Calvin, monopolized the evening. He
kept going on about life's ups and downs and all his needs.
Those listening would have been happy to help Calvin if he
had shown any concern for anyone else's need to share, but
the group kept silent as he droned on, ensuring even less
compassion in the room.

God commands us to humbly serve one another and to
share with those in need. We are to bear one another's
burdens. We should also share the difficulties we may be
experiencing, but in humility we defer to the needs of
others. Then God will grant you everything you need in life.

Grace upon Grace

Be generous to others and put them first.

Submit to Authority

Remind them to submit to rulers and authorities,
to obey, to be ready for every good work, to slander no one,
to avoid fighting, and to be kind,
always showing gentleness to all people.

TITUS 3:1-2 CSB

The list of considerations seemed overwhelming. To become a member of the organization, character and reputation had to be above reproach. To join, candidates had to submit to the group's authority, obey the written tenets, commit to hours of community service, be personable with others, and show kindness to all. The reward, however, was the joy of their relationships, shared work toward a common goal, and the knowledge that they would have a positive impact on their town.

As believers, we represent our Lord and Savior. We have been given the righteousness of Christ. We must submit to God, be students of the Word, and pray to see evidence of the fruit of the Spirit in our lives. As you interact with strangers, acquaintances, or family today, remember that you are an ambassador for Christ. Determine to make a difference with the way you live.

Grace upon Grace

Represent Christ to others so they may come to know him.

No Filter

If anyone among you thinks he is religious, and does not
bridle his tongue but deceives his own heart,
this one's religion is useless.

JAMES 1:26 NKJV

Bob loved to talk about his own accomplishments. He
advised people whether they wanted the advice or not, and
he offered his opinion on many subjects. Bob believed he
was helping people, but he wasn't actually any help at all. In
his mind he was an expert, but others saw him as a know-
it-all. Not much of what he offered was useful; it often was
just foolishness. Bob was the only one who valued his own
opinion, and although people listened and smiled, most
either resented or pitied him.

When we profess to be believers and then act in ways that
are harmful, prideful, or inconsiderate of others, we hurt
the cause of Christ. If we have no self-control, no filter
over what we say, or are careless about others' feelings,
we may even turn people away from faith in Jesus. May
our behavior lead others closer to redemption through
Jesus Christ by continually allowing him to guide us in
everything we say and do.

Grace upon Grace

*Consistently check your actions to be sure
they lead others to Christ's saving grace.*

Close Check

One who guards his mouth and his tongue,
Guards his soul from troubles.

PROVERBS 21:23 NASB

Martha knew it would be wrong to repeat what she had
been told. It hadn't been verified, but it sure sounded true.
Maybe she would just tell one friend. Martha would tell
Sandi, then make swear to secrecy, and she only confide the
most likely facts. Once Martha had spoken, however, she
felt a nudge in her spirit. She knew she had acted wrongly.
That was confirmed when the person she had gossiped
about came to her and let her know that everything she had
repeated was lies.

We need to keep a close check on the motives of our hearts
and the words that proceed from our mouths. When we
injure another person with hearsay, we bring judgment
upon ourselves. We must guard ourselves from any type
of speech that will bring harm, protecting ourselves in
the process.

Grace upon Grace

*Make sure the conversations you engage in bring glory
to God and benefit others.*

No Place

Let no corrupting talk come out of your mouths, but only
such as is good for building up, as fits the occasion, that it
may give grace to those who hear.

EPHESIANS 4:29 ESV

You could tell from Leila's words that she was filled with the
Holy Spirit. Her countenance conveyed that she was close
to Jesus' heart and had spent time at his feet. People flocked
to her because they left feeling encouraged and inspired.
Leila truly carried the life of Christ within her and blessed
everyone that she encountered.

When we determine that we want to sacrifice our lives for
Jesus in order to bring others to him, we must be aware of
the things we say and do. We need to be in his presence
continually through reading the Word and praying; then we
encounter people with a spirit of joy and the message of the
gospel. There is no place for coarse language or foul words.
Our mouths were made to praise and worship God and to
spread the good news.

Grace upon Grace

*Study, pray, and stay close to God,
and others will recognize Jesus in you.*

Avoid Wrath

An angry person stirs up conflict,
and a hot-tempered one increases rebellion.

PROVERBS 29:22 CSB

There was one couple, Don and Millie, on the block who
really needed to keep their windows shut because they
quarreled so often and so loudly. The tirade was intense.
A neighbor, Darius, spoke to them in a tender and sincere
request to consider the children on the street. People could
overhear their arguments. Unfortunately, this request
was met with an angry retort. Viewing Don and Millie's
disruptive behavior made everyone else on the block
determined to speak kindly to one another.

When we can diffuse a situation with a kind word, why
would we choose to speak harshly? We know better yet it's
tempting to get in that last, curt word. The consequences
when we speak without kindness can be monumental to
clean up. Avoid wrath, speak compassionately, and maintain
peace for your own good and for the benefit of others. By
doing this, you show Jesus to everyone that you know.

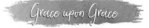

Grace upon Grace

*Think before you open your mouth and consider
the consequences of your words.*

Keeping Guard

God, give me grace to guard my lips
from speaking what is wrong.

PSALM 141:3 TPT

The foreign language class was provided with tape to place over their mouths for the first ten minutes of the period. They were to think of what they would say once the tape was removed. Their instructor cautioned them to carefully consider whether they were using the correct words for what they wanted to convey. They practiced mentally, agonizing over why they chose their specific jargon. The teacher warned that wrong usage would result in points detracted from their grade.

We don't get a report card for the words that proceed from our mouth, but we may forfeit the Lord's favor with carelessly harmful speech. Whether we are stating something regarding an instruction or just an opinion, we must do it in truth and with consideration for others. We are responsible for how our words affect those within our realm of influence. Before you utter anything, make certain your comments are delivered in truth with grace and love.

Grace upon Grace

*Remember that God is present in every conversation,
so keep a guard on your mouth.*

Words of Healing

Some people make cutting remarks,
but the words of the wise bring healing.

PROVERBS 12:18 NLT

The comedian's style was built on sarcasm. He would pick
a couple of people in the audience and roast them with
vigor. He held nothing back, believing he had a keen eye for
choosing those who could take it and not be offended. One
night, his perception was off, and he continually jabbed
a young woman who wasn't taking it well. When her buff
boyfriend noticed tears trickling down her cheeks, the
comedian felt the effects of his wrath.

Cutting remarks, even when spoken in jest, can do great
damage. The target may laugh on the outside, but on the
inside, they can be experiencing a lot of pain. Scripture
identifies the words of the wise as a healing balm to a
person's soul. Wisdom can speak into a situation at just
the right moment, bringing restoration and comfort to
a broken heart or a weary spirit. If we pray in faith for
wisdom, God promises to give it to us. Ask him so that you
can be the one who brings joy and restoration to someone
who need it in Jesus' name.

Grace upon Grace

Ask the Holy Spirit for wisdom to know what words to speak.

Words of Love

The soothing tongue is a tree of life,
but a perverse tongue crushes the spirit.

PROVERBS 15:4 NIV

For some people, childhood is full of the sweetest memories. They had supportive parents and family members who helped shape them into the person they are today. Others have a history they would rather forget. Maybe they had a father who always told them that they wouldn't amount to anything, or a mother who wondered why they couldn't be more like a sibling. If you had an unpleasant childhood, it does not have to define you today.

God loves you more than you can comprehend. It is a lavish love that exchanged the life of his only Son for you. If you have received Jesus as your Savior, you also have a home waiting for you with your heavenly Father in heaven. To him, you are his precious possession, a treasure, and his royal child. He sings over you and speaks words of love into your heart. Crushing memories of words spoken in your past need to stay in your past. Instead, dwell on what God says about you now.

Grace upon Grace

*When you feel that you're not good enough,
remember how God see you.*

Word Blessings

"What goes into someone's mouth does not defile them, but what comes out of their mouth, that is what defiles them."

MATTHEW 15:11 NIV

Bonnie was tired of being the joke of the lunchroom. The mean girls would taunt her about her restrictive diet and the strange foreign foods in her lunch kit. One day, Bonnie had had enough and was just about to hurl some of the detested food at the laughing group. She really wanted to add some choice words as well. She stopped, however, and remembered her mother's words—speak love and treat others as Jesus would treat them.

Our spiritual condition can be pure and holy or like dirty rags. When we conduct ourselves according to how Scripture instructs us, it speaks volumes about our maturity in Christ. It should mean everything to us to represent him so well that others want to surrender their lives to him. Don't be known as someone who defiles themselves with what comes from their mouths, but be one who speaks truth, love, and blessings.

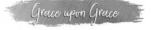

Grace upon Grace

Show others who Jesus is by the way you live.

Speak Love

Bless those who persecute you;
bless and do not curse.

ROMANS 12:14 CSB

It didn't make sense that Sally could be sweet to one
friend, yet cruel to another. What possessed her to shower
kindness on one person and deny it to someone else?
Jealousy. Feeling like the one woman's life was more blessed
than her own, Sally couldn't resist berating her.

If we truly trust God's sovereignty, then we should be
content with what he gives us and not envy what others
have. God always gives everyone his best, which will lead
to a closer relationship with him. He alone knows what we
need. Reacting in anger and envy and exhibiting malice is
sin. Scripture warns us that these things ought not to be.
Determine and pray that you will speak love and not curses
to those God has placed in your life.

Grace upon Grace

*Keep watch over your heart's intentions and the words
that proceed from your mouth.*

Confidence of a Friend

One who conceals an offense seeks love,
But one who repeats a matter separates close friends.

PROVERBS 17:9 NASB

Maisy overheard a conversation between two of her friends. She couldn't wait to repeat what she had heard. For a brief moment, she thought about being more Christlike by staying silent and just praying for the person who had spoken in private. However, if she spoke to other friends about it, they could pray too. Wouldn't Jesus want that— more prayer support? Her lack of wisdom won out and she spoke freely of what was shared confidentially. It cost her a friend and the trust of so many others.

Motives of the heart are deceptive when they are laced with sin. The enemy's voice always tries to fill us with doubt about the instructions in the Word and about God's will for us. When we hold the confidence of a friend close to our hearts and only speak of it to God in our prayers, we maintain the relationship. When we give way to sin and share what we were entrusted with or unintentionally privy to, we run the risk of losing our friends and a precious sister or brother in Christ.

Grace upon Grace

Pray for your friends and give counsel only through the guidance of the Holy Spirit.

All Powerful God

The LORD will fight for you;
you need only to be still.

EXODUS 14:14 NIV

Ashley panicked as she considered her options. How could she defend herself when Charlotte had framed her so convincingly? She couldn't compete when it came to Char's trickery, nor did she want to. Ashley's integrity made her an easy target. She did the only thing she knew to do; she went to the Lord in prayer and asked him to fight her battle for her. While she trusted in faith that he would fight for her, Ashley praised his name in advance for how he would faithfully defend her.

We serve a loving and all-powerful God who honors honesty and justice. When we act righteously in the face of an attack, the Lord is there to fight the war on our behalf. We don't need to do anything but continue to live in a godly way and in obedience to him. He will secure the win. In the interim, we should continue in faith, spending time in prayer and worship, believing without the shadow of a doubt that he will right every wrong. He will make truth shine out of the darkness.

Grace upon Grace

*Be still because the battle is the Lord's,
and he is always the victor!*

Good Counsel

The godly offer good counsel;
they teach right from wrong.

PSALM 37:30 NLT

When Agatha came to the counselor for advice, she expected to find quick help and an easy resolution to her issues. The therapist knew if help were given all in one session that Agatha would not return for a second appointment. He decided to draw things out, frugally doling out snippets of advice each time they met. There was always a missing nugget of information that would only be revealed at the next session. The process went on for months without any resolution, resulting in Agatha's inflated anguish, confusion, and cost.

When there's an ulterior motive there is always harm done. Without the regeneration of the Holy Spirit, the flesh only lives to please itself. Doing the right thing becomes understood for only Goody Two-shoes. As believers, we must always subscribe to truth. As we act with the best intentions and speak from righteousness, we will be trusted to give good and honest counsel to others.

Grace upon Grace

*Ask Jesus for purity of mind and heart
and seek wisdom from the Holy Spirit.*

Hear Others Out

The one who has knowledge restrains his words,
and one who keeps a cool head
is a person of understanding.

PROVERBS 17:27 CSB

The Rutger family had an annoying habit of speaking
over one another. When one of them would begin sharing
their thoughts, the rest were forming their responses in
their minds. They would then vocalize these ideas before
hearing the entirety of what was originally being said.
This resulted in retorts that made no sense and comments
that often didn't correspond very well with the gist of the
conversation. It might have been humorous had it not been
so exasperating. Eventually there were loud disagreements,
animosity, and misunderstandings.

If we would only have patience to truly hear someone when
they're speaking. We tend to rush to give our opinions
without allowing the other person to finish what they were
saying. Is that because we honor our own words far above
those of other people? Scripture tells us to pay attention to
what people are saying, consider their words, and not to
react with anger.

Grace upon Grace

*Be attentive in conversations,
showing concern for another's words.*

June

If he chose them by grace, it is
not for the things they have done.
If they could be made God's people
by what they did, God's gift of grace
would not really be a gift.

ROMANS 11:6 NCV

Hold Your Tongue

For lack of wood the fire goes out,
and where there is no whisperer, quarreling ceases.

PROVERBS 26:20 ESV

If you have ever played a game called telephone, you'll recall how the message whispered from ear to another was distorted by the time it got to the last person. It is evident that comments change based on the listener's interpretation of what they think they hear. This perceived message is usually altered or emphasized with unfounded emotions. Based on what is believed to be heard, reactions range from laughter to anger. This is the same with gossip. When it is passed from one person to the next it can be quite different. Once it makes its way back to the original speaker, relationships may be damaged offenses can occur.

Imagine if we lost any desire to ever pass anything along that could potentially damage another person? That would mean we would have to live in a world without sin. Since that is not the case, we should adhere to the Bible's instructions to never spread a false report. Speak only what will promote a life of peace with all people, avoiding angry confrontations that will never produce the righteousness of God.

Grace upon Grace

Practice holding your tongue instead of saying something that would cause others anguish.

Bridling the Body

We all stumble in many things.
If anyone does not stumble in word, he is a perfect man,
able also to bridle the whole body.

JAMES 3:2 NKJV

Samantha was the most eloquent speaker at church services
or gatherings. She knew her Bible and could readily
quote from it. She appeared to not only have a handle on
Scripture, but her deep faith was also reflected in the way
she lived. That was, until she was at a grocery store miles
away, unaware that another church member was also
there. Samantha was unhappy with the service and a blue
streak filled the air within earshot of the other congregant.
Her language revealed the truth of what was in her heart,
compared to the person she portrayed herself to be on
Sundays.

We all stumble; we all sin. Our tongues convey honestly
who we are on the inside. When we try to concoct a certain
persona for the purpose of being admired, eventually the
truth of who we really are will come to light. We should aim
to not only know the Word but to truly live it. Our mature
faith will be evidence of purity and righteousness.

Grace upon Grace

*Pursue maturity in Christ as you bridle your mouth
and your whole body.*

Respect and Grace

Let your speech always be gracious, seasoned with salt, so that you may know how you ought to answer each person.

COLOSSIANS 4:6 ESV

The situation was tense as co-workers Tatum and Terry bantered back and forth with accelerating volume. Once the boss, Mr. Channing, entered the room, however, you could hear a pin drop. The employees were all accustomed to the way he handled things with poise and decorum. As they waited for him to address the problem, they were confident that his answer would be wise, discerning, and clarifying. Both Tatum and Terry trusted him and when he spoke, everyone listened.

Sharing the gospel is the most important answer we will ever give to someone's spiritual inquiry. We should be well versed in our knowledge of Scripture so we can answer any question one might get. Our words should convey the greatest love, that of Jesus' life which was given in exchange for ours. We must be prepared to speak about the hope we have so that others will find salvation in Christ.

Grace upon Grace

Graciously share your testimony of salvation when an opportunity arises.

Bad Company

"I will watch my ways and keep my tongue from sin;
I will put a muzzle on my mouth
while in the presence of the wicked."

PSALM 39:1 NIV

Lionel was somewhat like a chameleon. Depending upon who was in his presence, his behavior would change. If he was with a church group, his actions were dictated by biblical standards. If he went for a drink with the guys from work, you wouldn't have recognized him. It didn't take Lionel long to settle in with the rowdy crowd and to emulate their behavior. It was a slippery slope, and sadly, he could switch gears in no time.

When we make friends with the world, we can be in danger of becoming more like them and less like Jesus. Our attitudes and language are often influenced by the company we keep. We must live in the world, but we are not to be like the world. Be wary of those with whom you associate. Share Jesus with the unsaved but make your closest friends those who are Christ followers.

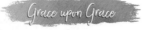

Grace upon Grace

Ask the Lord for wisdom to know who to pursue close relationships with.

Speak Spiritual Truth

A time to tear apart and a time to sew together;
A time to be silent and a time to speak.

ECCLESIASTES 3:7 NASB

Are you adept at reading the room? Can you tell when someone needs a cheery word or needs to be left alone? If we perceive our surroundings by the leading of the Holy Spirit, we can sense if someone needs prayer or encouragement. Speaking into a person's struggles and praising God with those who are rejoicing are both vital ministries. By seeking God's discernment, we can understand situations with his wisdom and his perfect timing.

We go through many seasons in life and God has a purpose for each one. We should pray for insight into how we respond to whatever the Lord brings our way. Our trials will teach us something that will allow us to minister to others in their challenging situations. We bless our brethren when we can testify that we experienced something similar to what they are now going through. Our ability to find spiritual truth during adversity can offer strength, hopefully providing a reason for them to endure.

Grace upon Grace

*Learn from your tribulations, so you can help others
in their time of conflict.*

Spread Blessings

The tongue has the power of life and death,
and those who love it will eat its fruit.

PROVERBS 18:21 NIV

The church group had had enough, and nervy Nick finally yelled, "Put your money where your mouth is!" The braggart, Simon, had waxed on for months about how his ideas would revolutionize the organization. He shared his visions of grandeur but never put any actions behind the plan. Initially the group had caught Simon's passion, but as time wore on, they realized that he was all talk.

When you compare the size of the tongue to other parts of the body, it seems small. The damage it can do, however, is enormous. When we promote ourselves and our own opinions, we can't take it back and people can't seem to forget it. God created our mouths to spread blessings and to praise him. We should use our words first and foremost to spread the good news of the gospel and to bring him glory.

Grace upon Grace

*Speak words of love, healing, and blessing
to turn others toward Christ.*

The Fight

Every kind of beast and bird, reptile and sea creature,
can be tamed and has been tamed by mankind,
but no human being can tame the tongue.
It is a restless evil, full of deadly poison.

JAMES 3:7-8 ESV

Pam and Paul had never had a fight like this one as the
words flew out of their mouths. They even shocked
themselves. They learned that evening that things can get
out of hand when there is no control over the tongue. There
were moments when they tried to hold back but it was as
if a dam had broken. They sat there in the aftermath of the
verbal wreckage, unable to retract what had been said and
not quite sure what they could do to repair it.

When you consider what Scripture says, it is impossible for
any of us to tame our tongues. That is quite horrifying. We
want to say it can't be true, yet we prove it all too often. To
combat it, we must fill our lives with his Word, his Spirit,
and all that is lovely. We will never be without sin on this
side of heaven, but we can surrender all that we are in order
to seek holy and righteous lives.

Grace upon Grace

*Keep watch over your tongue, controlling it
with the power of the Holy Spirit.*

Speak Worship and Praise

May the words of my mouth
and the meditation of my heart
be acceptable to you,
LORD, my rock and my Redeemer.

PSALM 19:14 CSB

Elise wrote the letter with the greatest of care, searching
for the perfect way to describe how she felt. She scattered
purposefully placed words of encouragement and heartfelt
compliments throughout. She desired the note to garner a
reaction, a devotion written in return. Elise hesitated before
sealing the envelope and whispered a prayer. She hoped that
revealing her affection would touch the soul of the reader.

When we use words to describe our love and appreciation
for our Lord, it blesses him. Our mouths should be filled to
overflowing with praise for him. Study his character in the
Word and praise him for each of his wonderful attributes.
Gratefully recall all he has saved you from. Remember that
he sacrificed his Son so you could live forever. Consider
his creation and his almighty works. Purposefully speak
worship and praise for his glorious name every day.

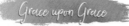

Grace upon Grace

Seek to glorify and please your loving, magnificent,
all-powerful God!

Remain Silent

Even a fool who keeps silent is considered wise;
when he closes his lips, he is deemed intelligent.

PROVERBS 17:28 ESV

Cole entered the room seeking respite from the wintery
weather. He didn't expect to wander into an academic debate.
He sat in the back of the room, just happy to have taken
refuge from the icy sidewalks. As Cole listened, he became
intrigued by the intelligent banter and lofty thoughts. He
considered the topic and had some comments of his own
since being on the street had given him quite an education.
He decided, though, to stay silent and just take it all in.

Most people who saw a street person like Cole probably
wondered who had let him in. If he had chosen to share
his thoughts, he might have had as much validity as the
professors themselves. Whether or not we are perceived as
intelligent enough to join a conversation, we should always
think about whether our interjections would provide a new
insight or be considered preposterous.

Grace upon Grace

*Use wisdom and discernment to know
when to be quiet and when to speak.*

Humanity's Punishment

Being found in appearance as a man, He humbled Himself by becoming obedient to the point of death: death on a cross.

PHILIPPIANS 2:8 NASB

The instructor, Mr. Ebbing, was late to class so a few of the students decided to take charge. They mocked their teacher, imitating him in insulting ways. They portrayed him as a bumbling, ridiculous caricature of authority. Just as Shane was levying the last joke at Mr. Ebbing's expense a timid student, Levi, stepped up to defend him. This caused the class to turn on Levi. He took on the humility of what had been intended for their teacher.

The greatest humility ever exhibited was which was done to the Son of God as he took humanity's punishment at Calvary. God became one of us, yet without sin. As the epitome of perfection, he died for all sin so we could be forgiven. He did nothing to deserve the torturous death that he endured. His desire for us to live forever with him overruled the drops of blood that he sweated and the lashes that he received. He took our place, died our deaths, and gave us everlasting salvation.

Grace upon Grace

Thank Jesus for his humble love and sacrificial death so that you can live.

Humility

He gives us more grace. That is why Scripture says:
"God opposes the proud but shows favor to the humble."

JAMES 4:6 NIV

There was a hidden prize in the cereal box. The twins
each wanted it. Amity drew the attention of her brother
elsewhere while she dug in the box hoping to snag the
treasure. Adam assumed that Amity would try to trick
him but didn't push the matter. Their mom watched from
a distance and figured this was a good teaching moment.
Entering the kitchen, she took the box and removed the
prize, giving it to Adam. When Amity fussed, she spoke
about humility and how each of us should consider others
ahead of ourselves.

God sees everything, both the good choices and the bad.
His favor falls on those who regard the welfare of others
first. His grace is abundant to any who care for their fellow
man before tending to their own needs. When we sacrifice,
ensuring that those around us benefit from our service, we
align ourselves with Christ. Jesus didn't look to his own
needs but to the world's. We're to follow his example.

Grace upon Grace

*Follow Christ's example of giving your life
for the benefit of others.*

Holiness

It is shameful even to mention
what the disobedient do in secret.

EPHESIANS 5:12 NIV

The Sorensen family carefully considered the reviews
before choosing a movie for Friday night. They baked the
pizza, and everyone settled in to watch the show. During
the first ten minutes of the film, however, they felt accosted
by the language and the violence that filled the screen.
Uncomfortable and convicted, they turned off the television
and had a conversation based on God's Word, about what
was acceptable and what was not.

We are called to be holy as God is holy. We should never
allow anything shameful to invade the privacy of our
homes, disguised as entertainment. To follow the direction
in today's verse, we must be careful about what we view and
listen to, for it all has an impact upon us. We will emulate
what we see. Guard your eyes and ears so that your heart
and mind are filled with what is true, pure, and righteous.

Grace upon Grace

*Consider the bad influences that media can have on you
and seek holiness.*

Falling Prey to Conceit

"Those who exalt themselves will be humbled,
and those who humble themselves will be exalted."

MATTHEW 23:12 NLT

Frederick Thompson was convinced that the county vote
would go in his favor. He had reviewed all the qualities of
his opponent, Barton Phelps, and considered them inferior
to what he had to offer. He even told his constituents that
he had the voting secured. They all noticed, however, that
his chest puffed up as he spoke of his anticipated success.
Across town, Mr. Phelps was spending hours making sure
he answered all the voters' questions and telling people that
if he were fortunate enough to win, he'd do everything he
could to serve them well.

Don't you think God would favor the humble politician?
It's in God's character to extol those who work on behalf of
others. When we think too highly of ourselves, we are likely
to be disappointed.

Grace upon Grace

Stay humble for God's service. Without him, you are nothing.

Company We Keep

> In the same way, you who are younger, be subject to the elders. All of you clothe yourselves with humility toward one another.
>
> 1 PETER 5:5 CSB

The two brothers, Andrew and Caleb, were always taught to respect adults, especially the elderly. Both valued their parents' teachings; at least that was the case until they entered high school. Caleb, however, started to hang around a bad crowd even though Andrew discouraged it. Eventually the head of the gang taunted Caleb to steal a grocery bag from an old lady. Wanting to look good in their eyes, he complied. When a policeman stepped out and caught him, all his new friends scattered.

Evil influence is lingering and ready to take hold of us. It often comes from the company we keep. If you desire to please people more than to honor God, that is where you have allowed a stronghold of sin. You place yourself in opposition to the Lord if you value your position in man's eyes more than you do in his. Submit in obedience to God, honor those in authority above you, and live humbly. This will allow your life to be filled with his grace.

Grace upon Grace

Care more about how God sees you than about pleasing man.

Others First

Do nothing from selfish ambition or conceit, but in humility count others more significant than yourselves.

PHILIPPIANS 2:3 ESV

Evelyn was a volunteer, and everyone considered her a ray of sunshine. She always took a back seat in order to allow other people their moments in the sun. Everyone wanted to be her friend, and she certainly denied no one. Even when it was rightfully her time to be honored, Evelyn would look around to see if there was someone she could also bring into the spotlight. When people asked her why she was so different, she told them about her Savior and how his love transformed her.

We all struggle; we find ourselves acting in ways we wish we wouldn't. We could be kinder, yet we revert to putting number one first. If we could fully grasp the blessings that come from putting others first, we would be doing it every day. If we desired the smile that graces our Father's face when he sees the behavior that is pleasing to him, we would surely alter our actions. Let us strive to silence any selfish desires and live to bless the people we encounter.

Grace upon Grace

*Ask for God's heart for people and a desire
to serve others ahead of yourself.*

Spiritual Heritage

Save your people, bless your possession,
shepherd them, and carry them forever.

PSALM 28:9 CSB

Nicolette spent hours collecting memorabilia and
photographs of family outings. She carefully digitized
the items she believed would be most cherished by every
member. As she recalled the times, good and bad, she
praised God for his faithfulness over the years. Marriages
that went the distance, babies prayed for and born,
baptisms, and those precious loved ones that had passed; it
was all there beautifully compiled: a testimony of their clan
to be viewed for years to come.

The Bible is our family history. From Adam to Abraham,
David to Jesus, it is our legacy. When you read the Bible
from this viewpoint, you have a new perspective—the
reality of ownership and belonging in every page. Every
record of prophecy that's been fulfilled or is yet to be, is
there to assure us that God will work to bring his children
together under the roof of his new kingdom.

Grace upon Grace

Understand how God's Word is your spiritual heritage.

Gentle Esteem

The reward of humility and the fear of the LORD
Are riches, honor, and life.

PROVERBS 22:4 NASB

Anna always showed discernment when reacting to a situation. She behaved with respect and demonstrated humility. How would her response improve on what was taking place? What comment or action would bring a righteous resolve and point people toward Jesus? Anna knew she was a representative of her heavenly Father; she had prioritized the glory and wonder of his name.

If we exist only for our own gain, our lives will be defined by the constant effort to fulfill selfish motives. If we maintain the goal of honoring God and serving his people above any consideration of ourselves, we can be certain we will receive spiritual blessing. Living for Jesus, following in his example of a humble and sacrificial servant will bring God's favor. Our time on earth is short, but eternity is forever. Store up experiences of putting Jesus first and live as he did, for your reward is in heaven.

Grace upon Grace

Try to serve God and others with a passion-filled, humble love.

All Else Pales

Keep your lives free from the love of money and be content
with what you have, because God has said, "Never will I
leave you; never will I forsake you."

HEBREWS 13:5 NIV

Ingrid tried not to bite her nails as she waited for the clerk
to get off the phone. When he swiped her credit card,
he looked at her questioningly and said that he received
a message to call the credit card company. Ingrid had a
feeling she knew why. Possibly it was that shopping spree
she had recently. "You really want me to do that?" the clerk
asked the person on the other end of the line. As he took
out some scissors and started to cut up her card, she knew
her spending had gone too far.

When we focus on Jesus and all the amazing things that are
to come in his kingdom, everything else pales. Desires for
earthly treasures fade when compared to the light of the
world. Isn't time spent with him far superior to anything
we could ever own or attain? He's with us always, loving us,
providing for us, answering our prayers, and fighting our
battles. He makes anything else we could want or desire
fade away.

Grace upon Grace

Consider Jesus to be all you want or need.

Stay Humble

A man's pride will bring him low,
But the humble in spirit will retain honor.

PROVERBS 29:23 NKJV

The embarrassment Sean felt as an employee was clear to everyone in the office as the flush spread over his face. He had been caught red-handed. He had just stolen a co-worker's report and had tried to pass it off as his own. Tim was on vacation when Sean saw the file on his desk. When no one was around, Sean took it and tweaked it to sound like his own. The ruse didn't last long though. When Tim returned to work, it was revealed that what was on his desk was a copy. He had already turned the project in to their boss.

When we want what someone else has, our desires and jealousies can only have destructive consequences. When our pride moves us to act foolishly and it is brought to light, we are certain to experience humiliation. Avoid covetousness at all costs. Stay humble and repentant of any jealousy. In following this process sincerely, we will find God's favor.

Grace upon Grace

Remain humble to live in the light of God's favor.

Hide It in Your Heart

Humble yourselves before the Lord,
and he will lift you up in honor.

JAMES 4:10 NLT

It was like the caricature of the angel on one shoulder and the devil on the other. Ellen heard the whispering in her ears, and she was leaning toward listening to the wrong advice. There was a strong urge to jump up and remind everyone that the idea was originally hers and hers alone. Someone should recall that Ellen had mentioned it first and she deserved the recognition. Or as the angel would recommend, Ellen could entrust it to God and be at peace, knowing that if he wanted it to be known, it would be.

We all have moments when we want to be recognized for something meaningful we have done. Or we could do what Mary did and hide things of this nature in our hearts, having faith that if God chooses to lift us up, he will. Really, it should be enough that God sees our right choices and our personal victories. He loves to give good gifts to his children and at the right time, he will reward you for those times you kept quiet about your own accomplishments.

Grace upon Grace

*Be content knowing that God sees everything
and will exalt you for his glory.*

Walk in Tandem

"Take up my yoke and learn from me, because I am lowly and humble in heart, and you will find rest for your souls."

MATTHEW 11:29 CSB

Liam was pleasantly shocked when he was approached with an opportunity from his professor. The prof was looking for someone to mentor, someone to whom he could impart his knowledge. It was overwhelming yet rewarding that Liam would be learning and working with such a brilliant instructor. He felt assured that this would help him make great strides in his career as he gleaned knowledge from such a frontrunner in the field.

Jesus' invitation is to take his yoke upon ourselves. We are to gain instruction from him as we walk in tandem with him. This will allow us to find true rest. The ultimate peace comes in the gift of salvation for we no longer need to strive against sin; it has been paid forever and for everyone. We don't need to work for our own redemption or achieve a high position. We don't need to prove anything for there is nothing we can do; Christ did it all. You will find rest for your soul as you walk alongside him.

Grace upon Grace

Be close to Jesus' side and experience the rest that comes from knowing him.

Count on a Downfall

Pride comes before destruction,
and an arrogant spirit before a fall.

PROVERBS 16:18 CSB

Rudy had just been awarded the position of head cheerleader, so she took her place in front of the squad. She commented that she thought herself the best person for the job, and she pulled out a mirror to apply her lip gloss before bounding out to the stadium to lead the cheers. The other cheerleaders watched her exhibit superiority until she tripped over her shoelaces and landed on her face. The crowd gasped, a few laughed, and Rudy found herself quite humbled by the experience.

When we get too full of ourselves, we can count on a downfall approaching soon. God hates pride and won't allow his children to remain in it. His great desire for us is that we be more like his Son. Jesus was the epitome of humility, taking on the likeness of man so that he could save us from our sins. When we pat ourselves on the back more than we praise God, we are foolish. To experience God's favor we must remain modest, remembering that without him we can do nothing.

Grace upon Grace

Stop and remember that without Jesus, you can do nothing.

Any Truth

"With the judgment you pronounce you will be judged,
and with the measure you use it will be measured to you."

MATTHEW 7:2 ESV

The rumors were buzzing and the person at the helm was no surprise. Sarah was always at the center of any hearsay so she could inform as many people as she could about the so-called news. She often didn't even have anything to verify her stories. Sarah, herself, decided who was at fault before she had the facts. When her conclusions turned out to be wrong, things started to fall back on her. People labeled her a gossip and commented that she could not be believed. Sarah was left with no one trusting her and no one to confide in.

We should always check our motives before we enter any conversation. We must consider why things are being reported the way they are and whether there is any truth to it. Is the conversation helpful? Would we say these words if the person being discussed was present? How would we feel if someone said the same things about us? We need to consider that slander and gossip are sins, and no believer should partake in that sort of conversation.

Grace upon Grace

*The Father can help you guard your tongue
and only say what is true and edifying.*

Collective Prayer

Confess your sins to one another and pray for one another, so that you may be healed. The prayer of a righteous person is very powerful in its effect.

JAMES 5:16 CSB

The women gathered around Katrina, who was upset and crying. They laid their hands on her shoulders. They prayed in such a heartfelt and intense manner that it was palpable. The Holy Spirit's presence was obvious to everyone, and an indescribable peace came over the room. Katrina's sobbing started to subside, and she felt a release that she had been seeking for months. This was all because of the fervent, loving prayers that were spoken over her by her sisters in Christ.

We are called to prayer, individually and in community. The gift of being able to go before the throne of God collectively for our sister in need is a great blessing for the recipient. As the righteous in Christ gather around to pray, there is power as the Lord answers. It doesn't matter if it is a confession, a health issue, or a need, the Lord hears when we intercede for one another. He works all things together for good, showing himself faithful to all.

Grace upon Grace

Count it a privilege to come before the Lord in prayer and seek his will.

Holy and Pleasing

In view of the mercies of God, I urge you to present your
bodies as a living sacrifice, holy and pleasing to God;
this is your true worship.

ROMANS 12:1 CSB

The teen girls' shopping trip was timed to occur just before
summer church camp. They needed some personal items
and maybe some fun outfits. Dawn and Adele were excited
about the lake, waterskiing, and blob jumping, so they
decided to check out the season's new bathing suits. Most of
the girls in the youth group had chosen modestly for their
swimsuits, but Dawn went in the opposite direction. Adele
reminded Dawn about how their appearances could be
problematic. Her gentle reprimand was met with humility.

Whether you're fifteen or fifty, what you choose to wear can
cause temptation for other members of the body of Christ.
Ask yourself what you're trying to achieve by wearing
something inappropriate or revealing. If your motive isn't to
encourage another believer toward purity, then it's time for
a fashion statement change.

Grace upon Grace

*Consider how the choices in your appearance honor God
and affect others.*

Trust Him

Humble yourselves, therefore, under the mighty hand of
God so that at the proper time he may exalt you.

1 PETER 5:6 ESV

Have you ever tried to make advancements and never quite
accomplished it? You start to realize that no matter how
hard you try, you just can't seem to move the needle. For a
believer, maybe it is due to God's training and preparation
for what he has in store. It's possibly just a timing issue.
Either way, God is at work in unseen places with a good
reason for holding a door closed.

In those times, can you trust him? Do you really believe
that he is working for your best? Rest in knowing that he
will fulfill the purpose he designed you for before you were
even born. Be confident in faith that at the right time, he
will open the door that he wants you to walk through to
carry out his will.

Grace upon Grace

*Walk in faith and gratitude while God is completing
the purpose he created for you.*

Good Fruit

"Blessed are the gentle,
for they will inherit the earth."

MATTHEW 5:5 NASB

Little Tammy was told many times to be gentle with the
baby. She had expected the baby to come home from the
hospital ready to play. Tammy didn't understand why the
infant was so tiny and all the baby did was eat and sleep.
Her mama tried to ease her disappointment by saying, "Just
be patient, for someday your little brother will be big like
you, able to run and do all the things you do." It helped the
bigger child look forward to what was to come.

Those who know Jesus and are being made into his image
have not reached perfection. There is the promise that one
day when we see him, we will be like him. In the meantime,
the Holy Spirit is creating good fruit in us, developing
gentleness, love, joy, kindness, and other fruit of the Spirit.
At the second coming, along with the new earth and our
new bodies, we will inherit all that God has promised to us
in Christ Jesus.

Grace upon Grace

Allow Jesus to grow the gifts of his Spirit in you.

Forgive One Another

Judgment is without mercy to the one who has not shown
mercy. Mercy triumphs over judgment.

JAMES 2:13 CSB

As a mom, Francis had had enough of her kids bickering
with one another. She figured, however, that she had come
up with the perfect solution. After the kids had been
fighting about every little thing and yelling that they never
wanted to see each other again, she took out their dad's
t-shirt. She made them put it on and wear it together,
outside arms each in a sleeve and inside arms at each
other's side. The two children couldn't escape each other's
presence. They had to figure out how to get along because
they were literally stuck with one another.

People are everywhere we go, and we must learn to get
along. Offenses will come because we are human, but
what we do when we are offended really matters. We must
forgive, even if we are not asked for forgiveness. If we want
God to forgive us, then his Word commands that we forgive
others. God wants us to understand the importance of
forgiveness. It brings freedom to us and to the offender, and
it covers us all in his grace.

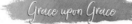

Grace upon Grace

*Fill up on God's love for others, so that you can be
quick to show mercy.*

Bow the Knee

"If My people who are called by My name will humble themselves, and pray and seek My face, and turn from their wicked ways, then I will hear from heaven, and will forgive their sin and heal their land."

2 CHRONICLES 7:14 NKJV

How would the farmers ever reconcile the damage done? The fields they had just planted and hoped to reap in the autumn appeared to be covered in water. It didn't seem like there was any way to rescue the baby seedlings. The missionaries invited the villagers to gather before the Lord and to pray for his mercy. As they bowed their heads and cried out to God, he graciously held back the rain and sent a warm wind. The next morning, the land was drier, and they could even see the small sprouts. "Praise to God!" resounded throughout the village that day.

Scripture tells us if we will humble ourselves, confess our sins, and petition the Lord, he will relent. He hears from heaven and is powerful enough to heal any plague. We are his servants and must bow our knees. We are also his precious children whom he adores. It is a divine mystery how it all works, and we are most privileged to be chosen.

Grace upon Grace

Bow before God in humility and ask him to revive your heart.

Stirred to Anger

A fool is quick-tempered,
but a wise person stays calm when insulted.

PROVERBS 12:16 NLT

If the boss encountered almost anything that upset him, he would explode. Mr. McLeod could go from zero to full speed if anything got under his skin. There was one person in the office, however, who could diffuse the explosion. Aaron was a mild-mannered, peace-keeping individual. He was not a doormat but an olive branch. He had the ability to bring serenity and calmness to any situation.

Some people equate a strong-willed, vocal person with power. They also often view a quiet, reserved person as weak. The Bible says that anyone who is stirred up to anger hurriedly is ignorant but one who is prudent keeps their cool. The person who can restrain themselves and show self-control is considered by the Lord to be wise. Always value and pursue self-discipline and discretion. Desire to live a controlled, God-honoring life.

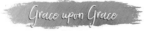

Grace upon Grace

*Exhibit the fruit of the Spirit, never seeking revenge
or showing hostility.*

July

Remember this:
sin will not conquer you,
for God already has!
You are not governed by law
but governed by the reign
of the grace of God.

ROMANS 6:14 TPT

Time to Own It

As God's chosen people, holy and dearly loved,
clothe yourselves with compassion, kindness,
humility, gentleness and patience.

COLOSSIANS 3:12 NIV

Life in this crazy, hectic world can tend to be so rushed
that we forget simple manners. Think about your response
the last time you got cut off in traffic, or the reaction you
got from another driver if you dared to honk your horn.
The stress of everyday life can make us react quickly and
sometimes downright rudely. This is not how it ought to be
for those who are in Christ. We have been given a better way.

We are chosen, endowed with spiritual gifts and the
indwelling of the Holy Spirit. Let that sink in and
understand that if you haven't yet, it is time to own it! You
have all you need in his Spirit to be compassionate, kind,
humble, loving, and restrained. You can discipline yourself
to have responses that don't erupt with irritation and angry
actions. We must all be clothed with these attributes in
order to glorify Christ in our lives. Through his power, they
are fully available to us.

Grace upon Grace

Honor Christ with the way you live.

Only Through Christ

When arrogance comes, disgrace follows,
but with humility comes wisdom.

PROVERBS 11:2 CSB

Everyone in the office could see it coming. They wished they had a way to halt the runaway train of Shawn's arrogance. Each little success went straight to his head, causing him to share exaggerated boasts. He was so busy singing his own praises that he neglected to fulfill a time-sensitive obligation for the CEO. When the project didn't arrive on the big boss's desk on schedule, he was livid. Shawn's ego was quickly deflated when his boss called him on the carpet for foolishly ignoring his proper duties.

Jesus said that apart from him, we can do nothing. Wouldn't it be wonderful if any time we achieved an honor we immediately whispered an acknowledgement to Christ for enabling us? We should always thank the source of our abilities. We can be confident knowing that all things are possible with Jesus, never letting that assurance morph into self-pride. Let's go forward, knowing that only through Christ can we do all things.

Grace upon Grace

*Seek his power in humility because
with Christ all things are possible.*

Sharing Wisdom

Who among you is wise and understanding? By his good conduct he should show that his works are done in the gentleness that comes from wisdom.

JAMES 3:13 CSB

People approached Pia's door with the hope they might experience one of her pearls of wisdom. Her door was always open to share nuggets of truth, and her arms were always ready to give a warm hug. Pia had lived a life riddled with trials and hardships, and this had produced unparalleled insight and humility in her. She was generous with her time, realizing it was her responsibility and honor to share what Jesus had taught Pia since he had been her constant companion throughout her life.

Sometimes we learn great truths through good times but more often the deeper lessons come from painful experiences. It's probably because we run to God more readily and desperately when we are suffering than during times of ease. We need to use our experiences to encourage and counsel others in their times of distress. We should generously share the understanding and knowledge we gain, surviving and thriving as a child of the King.

Grace upon Grace

Share what God has taught you in times of difficulty.

Set Free

"If the Son sets you free,
you will be free indeed."

JOHN 8:36 ESV

Jim and Karen sat looking at the bills wondering how they accumulated such a large debt. Maybe it was time to ask their bosses for raises? As they reviewed some of the bills more closely, they realized they had indulged in some extravagances. The only way for them to find freedom from the crushing financial burden was to curtail their spending and live within their means. As they exerted self-control, Jim and Karen found that their expenditures lessened, and peace was restored in their lives.

We had a debt for which we were incapable of ever making restitution. Our sins were so heinous, so extreme, that we were past the point of no return until Jesus stepped in. God, knowing there was no possible way for us to redeem ourselves, sent his only Son to pay the price on our heads. Through his cross and by our confessions, we are given a free pass for forgiveness of all our trespasses. We gain entrance into eternal life. The costliest act of love and sacrifice has provided for us freedom from sin and death.

Grace upon Grace

Give your whole heart and life to service for God.

Abundant Grace

He mocks those who mock
but gives grace to the humble.

PROVERBS 3:34 CSB

The city council listened to both sides of the argument in order to make the best decision. The group of businesspeople fought for more leniency to allow some questionable businesses into their city. The other group comprised of a local pastor, parents, and some seniors. They explained why this would be a threat to their community and detrimental to the wellbeing of their children. The greedy business entrepreneurs dug in their heels and protested that those people did not want the town to progress. However, the council could see the true motivation of the latter group and thought it best to side with the people who had presented empirical concerns and healthy motives.

God is never on the side of the self-important or people who only consider their own interests. The warning is evident—those who are self-centered will suffer the consequences of their greed, but those who are humble will experience the grace and blessing of their heavenly Father.

Grace upon Grace

Stay humble to experience God's grace, favor, and approval.

Search Your Heart

"I the LORD search the heart and examine the mind,
to reward each person according to their conduct,
according to what their deeds deserve."

Keeping a secret can be likened to a boiling pot: if you don't keep a closed lid on it, it might spill out. When keeping a confidence, emotions and poor motives can tempt us to share what is not ours to reveal. The enemy twists our thinking into believing that we're doing the one who confided in us a favor. Satan convinces us to share so others can know and pray about the concern. If we act upon the temptation, it leads to gossiping in the guise of alarm. We're then certain to find ourselves suffering the consequences, whether it is the loss of a friendship or the distrust of others.

As the Lord searches our hearts and minds, we should seriously consider our intentions. We should ask ourselves questions such as, "Should we repeat this information and will sharing it help or hurt?" Most importantly, "Why am I sharing something entrusted to me in confidence?" God is watching and he will rebuke or reward. Remember that your deeds, good or bad, will find you out.

Grace upon Grace

Search your heart so you can make wise choices.

What Is Right

Every way of a man is right in his own eyes,
But the LORD weighs the hearts.

PROVERBS 21:2 NKJV

We can justify almost anything if we want it badly enough. We find ourselves telling little white lies to explain away a sticky situation. On a shopping spree meant only for looking and not buying, we convince ourselves that we really need that one item. No one's name is on the yogurt in the fridge at work so there's no reason to ask; it must be up for grabs. Better to ask forgiveness than permission, right?

There are many ways we excuse poor behavior, convincing ourselves that it's okay. If we're honest, we'd admit that we have a red flag in our spirit yelling, "Danger! Do not proceed!" If we avoid demanding upright behavior from ourselves, the Lord will still be taking an account of our ways. He may even intercept us for our own good. Through correction, he will set our feet on the right path. Search your heart and avoid the need for discipline by deciding to do what is right in God's eyes.

Grace upon Grace

Examine your motives so you can live righteously for the Lord.

Allegiance

Obviously, I'm not trying to win the approval of people,
but of God. If pleasing people were my goal,
I would not be Christ's servant.

GALATIANS 1:10 NLT

Addy respectfully would not alter her mindset. She
knew what the right thing to do was and all the coercing
wouldn't change anything. Even the threat that she would
be an outcast didn't faze her. She had decided for Christ
long ago and her allegiance was to him. If the rest of
the world rejected her, Addy still wouldn't budge. Jesus
was her everything; anything and everyone else paled in
comparison.

It's hard to not fit in. We want people to like us and to
be our friends. We must be careful who we are trying to
win over though. If we have to deny our beliefs or our
obedience to God in order to belong to the crowd, we are
better off alone. Once a heart is given to Jesus, he places a
call on that life to live differently. We're not of this world;
we're heaven's residents. If you haven't yet, transfer your
citizenship to heaven and live like a real representative of
your true home.

Grace upon Grace

*Set goals to avoid the trappings of this world
and to live like a citizen of heaven.*

One Task

Just as we have been approved by God to be entrusted with a gospel, so we speak, not to please people, but rather God, who examines our hearts.

1 THESSALONIANS 2:4 CSB

Tallulah woke up with a start, reeling from a nightmare. People she socialized with but had never shared the gospel with were at the judgment seat of Christ. As they were being cast out, they turned to her and said, "We spent so much time together, why didn't you ever tell me? Why didn't you share Jesus with me?" Tears streamed down her face. Getting out of bed and on her knees, she asked Jesus to give her boldness and an urgency to share his good news.

We were given a task—to fulfill the great commission. We must ask ourselves how we are doing with that assignment. If we've not made it a regular activity, there is still time. There is not a minute to waste. God left us with the job of telling the world about his great love. What are we hesitating for?

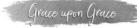

Grace upon Grace

Make the task of sharing the gospel a top priority.

Great and Mysterious

"Call to me and I will answer you, and will tell you great
and hidden things that you have not known."

JEREMIAH 33:3 ESV

Tom watched Prue as she came into the coffee shop each
morning, and he found her more beautiful every time.
When he finally got up the nerve to approach her, he found
that not only was she lovely on the outside but on the inside
as well. Prue was smart, fun, and kindhearted. Tom was
thrilled he had spoken to her because all he imagined about
her was surpassed, and a friendship of the deepest kind
began to grow.

God is the one who invites us to call out to him. He
promises in his Word if we do so he will answer us. Wow,
this is the Creator of the world we are talking about. There
is his promise to whisper unheard mysterious things from
his heart to ours. How in the world can we ever refuse
that? What an unimaginable privilege that God will share
intimacies with us. His great love and desire for us is
beyond comprehension, but it is sincerely real.

Grace upon Grace

Listen for the Lord's voice whispering to you.

Others First

Submit to one another out of reverence for Christ.

EPHESIANS 5:21 NLT

As Kate, Mila, and Callie filed through the long lunch line, their eyes fell on the menu for the day. The dessert was the favorite of all three kids. As they all chattered about how much they loved it, they were almost salivating. Kate and Callie grabbed the dessert but when Mila got there, they had run out. Seeing her friend's disappointment, Callie handed her dessert over. So touched, Mila said, "Why don't we share?" They realized that not only were their stomachs satisfied but their hearts were full as well.

There is a reason Scripture tells us to be humble and to consider others before ourselves. It is because when we do, we emulate Jesus. It blesses those around us, fills us with the love of Christ, and gives us an assurance that our Father is pleased. When we put others first, it is a chance for them to see Jesus in us. It's an opportunity to rejoice, knowing that most of all we wanted to please our Savior.

Grace upon Grace

Even though it requires sacrifice, put others first as Christ did.

True Faith

The goal of this command is love, which comes from a pure
heart and a good conscience and a sincere faith.

1 TIMOTHY 1:5 NIV

The speaker, Mrs. Trimble, admonished the women's group,
but not to cause those new in their faith to stumble. She
assured them that she was not accusing them of anything,
knowing their love for Jesus, but to remind them to think
about their actions. "Be aware of your enemy's schemes,"
she said, "and count the cost of how a poor choice may be
copied by a person who is spiritually immature." Remember
that Scripture says to act respectably, be modest and have
self-control. Those who have recently come to Jesus are
watching you and will learn from what you do.

We do have a responsibility to God to represent him
well, disciple those new in the faith and to live a life of
righteousness through Christ. Thankfully, we have the
anointing and power of the Holy Spirit to work in us. If we
stay in his Word by committing it to memory and instilling
it into our daily lives, we will be transformed into his
likeness. Inevitably with these efforts, our sincere faith will
show for all to see.

Grace upon Grace

*Purify your thoughts, actions, and words
so you exemplify Christ.*

Content of the Heart

The LORD said to Samuel, "Do not look at his appearance or at his physical stature, because I have refused him. For the LORD does not see as man sees; for man looks at the outward appearance, but the LORD looks at the heart."

1 SAMUEL 16:7 NKJV

The search for someone to be the face of the organization was infused with excitement. Applications were filled out by those who wanted the role. The position brought with it speaking engagements and media interviews. Many thought it was necessary to find both an intelligent spokesperson and a good-looking representative. Caitlin was gorgeous, but she lacked an insightful public presence. Everyone marveled when Reece got up because she spoke from a pure and lovely heart, revealing her unique beauty.

Aren't you glad that in a world of the disproportionate importance of appearances, God values what is on the inside? Man has such a skewed view of what is valuable, trading the content of the heart for body image. We all know that looks fade but the loving, considerate, and gentle heart of a godly woman shines eternally.

Grace upon Grace

Focus on what God values: the content of your heart.

Do Not Judge

Don't make judgments about anyone ahead of time—before the Lord returns. For he will bring our darkest secrets to light and will reveal our private motives. Then God will give to each one whatever praise is due.

1 CORINTHIANS 4:5 NLT

The parents' meeting had not started yet, but Sasha was busy canvassing the room about a program that she was presenting that evening. Sasha was seeking yes votes and was annoyingly persistent. She was afraid that some of the parents would disagree with her, and she spoke about her concerns as well as named the people she thought would oppose her. When those people arrived and the vote was called, they ended up supporting Sasha's program. She had maligned them falsely earlier in the evening and now was proven wrong. She felt quite embarrassed for spreading hearsay so prematurely.

We can't know what someone else is thinking or going to do unless they tell us. Why would we share something while in such ignorance? It only reveals our own foolishness. Let others speak for themselves. May we only say what benefits others and pleases God.

Grace upon Grace

Think the best of others; it's not your place to cast judgment but to extend grace.

The Lord's Battle

Don't be afraid of them,
for the LORD your God fights for you.

DEUTERONOMY 3:22 CSB

An unseen battle raged on even though nothing was visible.
Allie could feel a cold, eerie presence in the room. She had
experienced a spiritual victory and her mentor told her to
be aware that the enemy may strike after such a triumph. It
may have been her own fear that brought it on, or it could
have been an actual demon. Allie prayed, and empowered
by the Holy Spirit, she rebuked Satan. She reminded him
that Jesus was her defender and he had already won this war.

Whether it is a health, financial, relational, or spiritual
war, our God goes to the front line for us, and he is always
triumphant. All we need to do is trust, pray and rest in him.
As we exercise our faith, he really does have it all under
control. No one can compete with our Lord Almighty and
though Satan tries, he is nothing compared to our all-
powerful God. No matter what assails you, turn to your
deliverer, your heavenly Father, who will never allow you to
be overcome.

Grace upon Grace

*Trust that there's nothing to fear with the Lord
as your defender.*

A New Life

We are God's children now, and what we will be has not yet been revealed. We know that when he appears, we will be like him because we will see him as he is.

1 JOHN 3:2 CSB

Mira was disabled, and she really enjoyed watching children play from her front porch. She laughed with joy, remembering what it was like to be young. Mira knew exactly how it felt to run and play all day with endless amounts of energy. Oh, how she wished she could get up and join them and leave the constraints of her wheelchair. She longed to jump rope and play ball. She had been a good athlete and wished again for the days when her body did whatever she had wanted it to do.

Scripture says that when Jesus returns, we see him, and we will be changed. We don't know exactly what that will look like, but we do know that the Bible says there will be no more tears and no more pain. Regardless of what we will be, we will be like Jesus and there is nothing better. We are constrained to the limitations our present anatomical struggles within this life, but we are ordained for a new body, a new earth, and a paradise forever in God's kingdom.

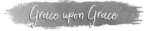

Grace upon Grace

Take heart that this life is not the end;
there will be a new beginning for you in heaven.

Run from Sin

"If you do well, will you not be accepted?
And if you do not do well, sin is crouching at the door.
Its desire is contrary to you, but you must rule over it."

GENESIS 4:7 ESV

Ava nervously bit her nails as she contemplated her choices.
She wanted to fit in at high school and have some fun
with the girls, but what about her parents? She knew they
wouldn't approve of these friends. They thought these girls
were quite wild. Her folks were on a trip, though, so they
wouldn't even know she had gone out with her friends.
When things at the mall got out of hand and the girls
coerced Ava into a car with some boys she'd never met, she
got a sick feeling in her stomach. Ava realized that she had
given in to sin and gotten herself into a dangerous situation.

Sin is not something to be trifled with for it eventually leads
to death. We have every instruction we need in Scripture to
help us avoid temptation. The indwelling of the Holy Spirit
gives us the power to say no. The suffering of our Savior on
the cross can influence us to stay as far away from evil as
possible. We must conquer our lusts and with the help of
Jesus, we have all we need to do so.

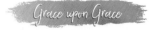

Grace upon Grace

*Develop a conscience that is so sensitive to sin
that you run from it immediately.*

Eyes on Jesus

Whatever you do in word or deed, do everything in the
name of the Lord Jesus, giving thanks through Him to God
the Father.

COLOSSIANS 3:17 NASB

Camila just felt stuck. There was the laundry, the grocery
shopping, and the never-ending cleaning. Being a mom
was so often monotonous and she felt like a robot. Camila
needed something to bring the passion back into her life.
When a friend invited her to Bible study, she certainly
didn't think that would be it, but she went for the lack of
another activity. It was there she found her purpose. Camila
met Jesus, and suddenly even the mundane tasks were
filled with joy. Having a clear purpose for the sake of the
kingdom changed everything.

Do you ever feel like you are just going through the
motions with everything on auto pilot? This life is about
Jesus and no matter what we do, we can do it with joy and
thanksgiving because of him. Things won't always be as
they are today. If we keep our eyes on Jesus and commit
to do our best in his name, we will add eternal value to
everything we do.

Grace upon Grace

Determine to do all things for Jesus,
and watch your days move from boring to blessed.

She Knew Jesus

"Do not be afraid of those who kill the body but cannot kill the soul. Rather, be afraid of the One who can destroy both soul and body in hell."

MATTHEW 10:28 NIV

Most of us know the story already. Two young men in long black coats and carrying guns walked into a high school and opened fire. When they came upon one of the students that they thought was religious, they asked her if she believed in Jesus. Having decided long ago that she would never deny him, the student said yes, that he was her Savior. Because of that answer her life ended there, and she went to heaven. Jesus welcomed her home.

We live in a scary world. It would be hard to go anywhere for fear of the violence we might encounter. We, however, know God is always with us. Before we were even born, he knew us. He never takes his eyes off of us, and nothing can touch us without his approval. We are not to fear man, only God. He has given us the gift of salvation and the way of escape from hell. The way is Jesus.

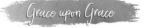

Grace upon Grace

Do not fear man because God holds your life in his trusted hands.

Slaves of Christ

Slaves, obey your earthly masters with deep respect and fear.
Serve them sincerely as you would serve Christ. Try to please
them all the time, not just when they are watching you. As
slaves of Christ, do the will of God with all your heart.

EPHESIANS 6:5-6 NLT

The fast-food restaurant was always busy. Mr. Glenn was
pleased, especially with Tony who was always hustling.
What Mr. Glenn didn't see was the slack that Megan picked
up for Tony when the owner wasn't there. Tony kept an
eye out for his boss' vehicle, and when he saw it, he put his
efforts into high gear. Megan labored diligently but was
overshadowed by the personality and fake elbow grease of
her co-worker. When Mr. Glenn left, Tony sat around lazily
and ordered Megan about their duties.

God's eyes are always on us. He sees when we're honest
workers and he sees when we take advantage of our
employment situation. If we respect our superiors and
value our work, we will be trustworthy. We are to serve our
employers as we would serve Christ. Everything we do on this
earth should be with the desire to present our duties to the
Lord in gratitude for the purposes he has placed in our lives.

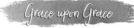
Grace upon Grace

Pay attention that you are not working for man but for God.

Savvy

"As for you, my son Solomon, know the God of your Father, and serve Him with a loyal heart and with a willing mind; for the LORD searches all hearts and understands all the intent of the thoughts. If you seek Him, He will be found by you; but if you forsake Him, He will cast you off forever."

1 CHRONICLES 28:9 NKJV

Harper considered her mom not very savvy. She "borrowed" her mom's credit card and charged stuff from a popular website, but she had it delivered to a friend's house so her mom wouldn't know. When the bill came her mom would tell the company that she never ordered it, and Harper could explain it away as a gift. She felt her plan was fail-safe until her friend's mom intercepted the package and called Harper's mom to let her know she could pick it up. Harper's shopping privileges were rescinded indefinitely.

At the onset of any temptation, we should go to God asking for his power to overcome the temptation. Consider the condition of your heart and make certain that you are committed to him, desiring to seek and obey him all of your days.

Grace upon Grace

May the desires of your heart and mind be pleasing to God as you seek him.

Stay Your Thoughts

Whatever is true, whatever is honorable, whatever is just, whatever is pure, whatever is lovely, whatever is commendable—if there is any moral excellence and if there is anything praiseworthy—dwell on these things.

PHILIPPIANS 4:8 CSB

Being at a performance of Chloe's left you feeling like you were in an uplifting animated musical with singing birds and happy sunshine. People flocked to her; many wanted to be her. Chloe didn't focus on that though, but on filling her mind with joy over the one who made her the way she was. Her heart and soul belonged to Jesus, and because of her humble spirit and spiritual determination Chloe made an impression on people that left an indelible impact.

Maybe the reason God instructs us to think truthful, honorable, pure, and praiseworthy thoughts is because of the propensity toward depression and sorrow in so many lives. He knows the mind is a battleground and that staying our thoughts on lovely things will help defeat the enemy. If you are struggling today with lies from the pit, remember to whom you belong, put on your praise music, get out the Word, and worship God in everything you say and do.

Grace upon Grace

Think on praiseworthy things and remember what a joy it is to belong to Christ.

No Hidden Agenda

Never once did we try to win you with flattery, as you well
know. And God is our witness that we were not pretending
to be your friends just to get your money!

1 Thessalonians 2:5 NLT

The new family at church had been blessed with many
luxuries, a booming business, and a gorgeous home on
the lake. Madison became aware of the Brabant family's
extravagant belongings, and she felt immediately drawn to
them. She made herself available to help them with anything
they might need. Madison didn't fully acknowledge her
motives, but deep in her heart she wanted to be invited to
enjoy some of the perks of their lifestyle. Her adulation for
them was inauthentic and for her own benefit.

The disciples in the early church had one motive: to
spread the gospel. They weren't trying to make a name for
themselves or pocket the offering. They were seeking God's
favor through their service, humbly committing their lives
to his glory. They were upright and honest with no hidden
agenda. Their only goal was to see lives won for Christ. We
should do the same.

Grace upon Grace

*May the good news be on the tip of your tongue—
ready to share with others.*

Battle of the Brothers

"Everyone who is angry with his brother will be liable to judgment; whoever insults his brother will be liable to the council; and whoever says, 'You fool!' will be liable to the hell of fire."

MATTHEW 5:22 ESV

Norman and Conan were inseparable when they were little but as they grew older, they developed different interests. They disapproved of each other and struggled to understand what the attraction was for the different pastimes. When Norman created a project for school from his beloved hobby, Conan ridiculed it. First, they had a verbal fight, but then it became physical. It ended with the project being broken to pieces. Both boys were suspended and warned that they had to find a way to get along.

Not everyone is going to like each other enough to be close buddies, but we are called to love one another. We might interact with a brother or sister for a season to help them in a time of difficulty or to mentor them in their walk, but that doesn't mean we will spend every waking moment with them. While we are in each other's presence, we are to show kindness and deference to one another.

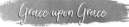

Grace upon Grace

Try hard to unconditionally love everyone God has placed in your life.

Mercy and Provision

My God will supply all your needs
according to His riches in glory in Christ Jesus.

PHILIPPIANS 4:19 NASB

Hazel looked at the empty cupboard and fear started to rise in her heart. Her hours at work had been cut and she found it increasingly tough to provide for her two children as a single mom. One day when Hazel had to decide whether to spend her last few dollars feeding her children or buying medicine for herself, she sobbed. She petitioned God for mercy and provision. Soon someone from church showed up with several bags of groceries. Then work called saying they were able to reinstate Hazel's hours. Her tears flowed again, but this time it was from gratitude for her Savior.

God promises to provide for us. Sometimes when it seems like there is no hope, he is already at work on the answer. We must trust that he will be faithful, he is aware of what we are lacking, and he will never leave us or forsake us. Our ways are not his, nor are our thoughts so when we don't understand the worst of times, we must wait and believe. He will always come through with his perfect timing.

Grace upon Grace

Trust that God knows what you need better than you do.

Asking Wrongly

You ask and don't receive because you ask with wrong motives, so that you may spend it on your pleasures.

JAMES 4:3 CSB

Arie practiced what he would say to his parents when he asked for money for the school ski trip. He was aware that a few of the kids were planning to sneak out after curfew and go night skiing. Because of this, Arie increased the amount he was asking for. He hoped his insecurity and fibbing wouldn't surface and betray his objective. Unaware that his parents had already spoken to the school and knew the exact amount needed for the outing, Arie insisted that the price he was telling them was correct. When they leveled with him about what they knew, he was not only denied the money, but was forbidden to go on the trip as well.

When we devise dishonest ways to feed our deceitful desires, we are likely to be discovered. Scripture says if we ask wrongly, we will not be given what we request. We will be denied when we ask for sinful pleasures. God sees the intentions of our hearts. He will not give us anything that will allow us to continue to sin.

Grace upon Grace

Check your motives and be careful not to ask for anything that will hinder you.

Good Intentions

God will never be mocked! For what you plant will always
be the very thing you harvest.

GALATIANS 6:7 TPT

Lucy knew her best friend was interested in a certain young
man, and he returned the feelings. Unfortunately, she
shared the same attraction as her bestie. She gave a party
and invited both of them, hoping to see if he might return
her feelings. It was a despicable thing to do, but she was
helplessly drawn to him. When they arrived, she flirted, and
her friend noticed. When asked why she would do such
a thing, she confessed her feelings and intent, losing her
friend and the respect of the young man.

When we use deceptive means to try to get what we want,
we usually end up losing. Plotting harm against others to
advance our interests never pleases God. Because he loves
us, he will make sure we learn our lesson in hopes that
we don't repeat the act. Remember that God sees into the
depths of your heart. Make sure the sight he sees is one of
purity and the best intentions.

Grace upon Grace

Pray for a pure heart, a righteous spirit,
and good intentions in all that you do.

The Word

The word of God is living and active, sharper than any two-edged sword, piercing to the division of soul and of spirit, of joints and of marrow, and discerning the thoughts and intentions of the heart.

HEBREWS 4:12 ESV

The infected wound was created by a piece of metal that had wedged itself into Grace's arm. The area had swollen to twice its normal size and the pain was almost unbearable. The doctor took his scalpel and cut into the skin. His experienced hands went to work with meticulous skill. Once the physician and his scalpel had done their job, Grace could start healing and the damaged tissue could be surgically replaced.

The Bible is the only book ever written in which the words are alive. For those believers who commit to its study, the message jumps off the page and cuts into the heart. It tells of how God loves each of us. He heals his children, saves them, and matures them in Christ. The Bible keeps us from trespassing against God, teaches us wisdom and discernment for daily life, and leads us into life everlasting.

Grace upon Grace

Become a master of studying God's Word and live by it continually.

Desiring Man's Approval

Nor did we seek honor from people, either from you or from others, though we could have asserted our authority as apostles of Christ.

1 THESSALONIANS 2:6 NASB

Ben was the most educated in the room, yet he was the most silent. As the yet unannounced guest speaker, he listened as the attendees waxed on about their knowledge of the subject. Some complained as to why they needed to listen to this expert, since they were already so well versed in the topic. The professional could have interjected, defending his presence based on degrees and awards. Yet, he had confidence in what he had to share without needing their acknowledgment to substantiate it.

When sharing Christ, we don't need to speak of our studies or gain man's endorsement of our standing in the faith. We only need to share the gospel. The Holy Spirit will ignite our words to penetrate hearts and minds to see the truth. It's unimportant what anyone thinks of us, and eternally vital as to what they think of the Savior. Don't desire man's approval; you already have the adoration of the one who matters most.

Grace upon Grace

Share the gospel without concern of what man thinks of you.

Study Program

This is good, and pleases God our Savior, who wants all people to be saved and to come to a knowledge of the truth.

1 TIMOTHY 2:3-4 NIV

The opportunity to apply for the study program was offered to all the students. It was a privilege that, if awarded, would change the course of their education. It meant they would have to alter their current schedules, taking time to learn new educational strategies. Once they committed, they'd begin a rigorous journey. They would become so enlightened that their way of approaching their research would never be the same again.

God has revealed all we need for salvation in his Word. It tells the sacrifice of our Savior for the forgiveness of sins. It reveals a love so great that the Creator would become the created to atone for those he had made. The heart of the Father is for all to come to salvation. We are his messengers, charged with the commission to speak life. We don't know who will accept him and who won't, so we must share the good news with all.

Grace upon Grace

Be ready to give an account of what you believe.

Beyond Our Imaginations

To Him who is able to do exceedingly abundantly above all that we ask or think, according to the power that works in us, to Him be glory in the church by Christ Jesus to all generations, forever and ever. Amen.

EPHESIANS 3:20-21 NKJV

The audience was flabbergasted by the magician's performance. How could his sleight of hand seem so authentic? They knew a person couldn't just disappear, yet the explanation of the woman's sudden absence was beyond their imaginations. They cheered, but still asked each other how it could be done. When the showman made the woman reappear there was a palpable gasp, and everyone jumped to their feet applauding.

Most people don't really believe in magic, yet we live in a spiritual world filled with miraculous events of which we are mostly unaware. There is a darkness that tries to invade the light of Christ in our lives. And there is our Lord, who is always victorious and works continually on our behalf doing things that would boggle the mind of the godliest believer. We must pray, asking God to help us understand the extent of what our heavenly Father can do.

Grace upon Grace

Access the power of the Holy Spirit in order to fulfill God's will.

August

God still loved us with such great
love. He is so rich in compassion and
mercy. Even when we were dead and
doomed in our many sins, he united
us into the very life of Christ and
saved us by his wonderful grace!

EPHESIANS 2:4-5 TPT

Avoiding the Dilemma

Let the Holy Spirit guide your lives. Then you won't be
doing what your sinful nature craves.

GALATIANS 5:16 NLT

Lily wasn't going to put the candy in her cart, but a lack
of willpower won out. She convinced herself she would
only eat one piece a day. This wouldn't interfere with her
promise to herself to lose weight; that one little indulgence
would not make a difference. Unfortunately, one piece led
to another and before Lily even got home from the store
half the bag was gone.

It's a slippery slope when we play with sin. We think we can
teeter on the edge and not fall off. The truth is, we stand
on our own power when we entertain our lusts, yet we are
weak and defeated. We avoid this dilemma by surrendering
every day to the Holy Spirit when we are leaning toward
sin. This is how he can prick our consciences and realign
our motives. We are not left to our own devices unless we
choose to be. We have been given all we need for a godly
life through the knowledge of him who has called us to be
his own.

Grace upon Grace

*Surrender to the indwelling of the Holy Spirit
to receive victory over sin.*

Trustworthy

"You are the ones who justify yourselves in the sight of others, but God knows your hearts. For what is highly admired by people is revolting in God's sight."

LUKE 16:15 CSB

The investment group was whipped into a frenzy as the speaker explained the newest opportunity. They were ready to open their wallets. His description of the returns and the minimal knowledge needed on their part made it sound like an easily earned fortune. Best of all, his company would do all the legwork. Legal considerations were already prepared and all they had to do was give him their financial commitment, sign on the dotted line, and trust him.

Pray for discernment in order to determine the truth of what God sees in others. Are they trustworthy, people to whom we should link ourselves, or are there red flags about their character? If you are idolizing a certain individual or their heightened opportunities, then you are entering into sin. Ask God for wisdom. He will let you understand which people to align with and which to avoid. Scripture says we are known by those we associate with. Let most of you trust be for like-minded Christ followers.

Grace upon Grace

Ask God for wisdom to discern the honesty of another's heart.

Look at Yourself

"Judge not, that you be not judged."

MATTHEW 7:1 ESV

"What in the world could have possessed Layla to do such a foolish thing?" the older sister, Nova, asked. "We were raised better than that and we know the consequences of such actions." Layla had shared a family secret with someone who had betrayed her confidence. Now the whole community was buzzing. Nova continued to discuss her sister's folly with friends. Then she ran into an honest friend who reminded her in front of other people that Nova had also shared part of this secret, but enough for many to put two and two together. She should look at herself before blaming Layla.

Whenever we accuse others without looking at our own indiscretions, we place ourselves in danger of sinning. The truth always comes to light. If we can't see our own failings but view others' as if they were flashing neon signs, we deceive ourselves. We must review our own behavior before passing judgment on others. Show mercy and help those in the wrong find repentance and restoration. In that situation, you would hope they would do that for you.

Grace upon Grace

Avoid criticizing the sins of someone else when you have sins of your own.

Warning Signs

There is a way which seems right to a person,
But its end is the way of death.

PROVERBS 14:12 NASB

Elton was a high school football captain, and he and his girlfriend, Riley, were taking a walk on a hot summer night. Elton was talking about his opportunities for college scholarships and felt like celebrating at the ice cream shop. First though, he wanted to take a swim. His neighbors were on vacation, so their pool was open. Even though there was a warning sign to not enter, in the light of the moon, Elton dove in. Riley screamed, noticing the pool was empty. The warning sign was placed there because the pool was being painted. Elton broke his neck; any dreams of a sports career were doused.

God's Word warns us about the dangers of remaining in a life of sin. Scripture says that when sin is accomplished it brings forth death. God gives us his commandments to protect us, and his desire is always for our good. Obedience and dedication to know the Word and follow it will provide a safe and sure environment.

Grace upon Grace

Focus on living the purpose God has for you and follow him daily.

Our First fruits

Honor the LORD with your wealth,
with the firstfruits of all your crops;
then your barns will be filled to overflowing,
and your vats will brim over with new wine.

PROVERBS 3:9-10 NIV

The couple's success was enviable, yet Emilio and Willow
were so likable that people felt only admiration for them.
They never bragged about their possessions and were
always allowing other people to use their lake cabin or
enjoy their spacious family home. When Emilio and Willow
weren't working, people would find them helping at the
local shelter. If there was a volunteer needed at church, they
were always available. They honored God and served him
first, and he blessed them for it.

If it were not for the Lord, we would have nothing. It is
only by his generous hand that we enjoy our next breath, let
alone our family, our jobs, our homes, our health, and the
list goes on. Even when we honor him with our first fruits,
we are giving back to him what he has so generously given
to us. Give with a cheerful heart and trust God's provision.

Grace upon Grace

Give lavishly when you are met with a need.

Ending in Victory

When evening had come,
He sat down with the twelve.

MATTHEW 26:20 NKJV

Alton invited his parents and his siblings to dinner at his home. He planned to reveal some news after the meal. The atmosphere was festive. They treasured this time and were eager to celebrate whatever he was going to share. Alton stood when the food was gone and everyone was finished, and then he announced that he had sold everything he owned and was going to live in a foreign land to fulfill the Great Commission. They cried tears of sadness for themselves mixed with tears of joy for those who would hopefully be saved through his calling.

When Jesus ate the last supper with his disciples there was a myriad of emotions. Who would betray him? Where was he going, and could they go too? This first Passover was a time of sadness and rejoicing when the disciples made promises which were later broken. Yet it was a time of celebration, for it led to the cross, the resurrection, and Christ's victory over sin and death.

Grace upon Grace

When you sit down for supper, talk about Christ's victory over sin and the grave.

Mending Broken Hearts

The LORD is close to the brokenhearted;
he rescues those whose spirits are crushed.

PSALM 34:18 NLT

Denise's dream board adorned the wall in her office. She had hoped to gain entrance into one of the best colleges and was accepted. She worked hard to graduate with honors, and she achieved it. Knowing exactly which firm she wanted to work for, she was fully confident that the door would open. The interview went exceptionally well, and now all she needed to do was wait for the call announcing her employment. When a no was delivered, she bravely moved on to her second choice. When the third and sixth firm had turned her down, she could feel her heart break in her chest.

God had another plan. The young woman's talents would be used in ministry and the purpose he planned would bring her more fulfillment than all six firms would have. When she got on board with his plan, her wounded heart started to heal. When she realized that God had given her his best, her soul was mended fully, and the life he chose for her was better than she ever could have imagined.

Grace upon Grace

Fight against discouragement when your plans don't work out and seek God's perfect will.

What Was Lost

He heals the brokenhearted and binds up their wounds.

PSALM 147:3 NIV

The training was intense, but the prospect for Violet of running her first marathon was exhilarating for her as a new athlete. Every evening after work she went to the track, stretched, and ran. She changed her eating habits and monitored her water intake. When there were only five days left before the big event, Violet pushed a bit too hard and tore a muscle. The doctor said she would have to wait for the next race because her recovery would be at least a month. Not only were Violet's muscles affected but so was her heart.

When you work diligently toward a goal and it is taken from you, it can be devastating. If you take your brokenness to God and ask him to help you understand and deal with your new situation, he will do more than you can imagine. His power to heal emotionally and physically is unrivaled. His way of showing you his good plan through your suffering is the exact answer you need. He never allows anything to go unused. He will always redeem whatever you believe was lost and give it eternal meaning.

Grace upon Grace

Give God your broken heart, trusting him
to make beauty from the ashes.

His Acceptance

The sacrifice you desire is a broken spirit
You will not reject a broken and repentant heart, O God.

PSALM 51:17 NLT

John turned his head away when his parents questioned him about the dent in their car. They knew by his body language that he was guilty. They also knew his anxiety about confessing and that he was punishing himself already. However, John had been told not to take the car so there would be consequences. He finally turned and told the truth, taking full responsibility through his tears. His parents immediately forgave him and hugged him. Both parents told John how thankful they were that he was safe.

God waits for us to come to him and ask forgiveness. He will woo us to him, knowing that we may be fearful or believe that we are unforgivable. But that lie is from the enemy. When we fall at God's feet in repentance, he receives us like the father did the prodigal son. His open arms convey his acceptance. His Word convinces us that our sin has been washed white as snow. The slate is clean and our relationship with our heavenly Father is restored.

Grace upon Grace

You can go to the Lord with the ugliness of your sin and confess; he is never against you.

Constant Protection

Cast your burden on the LORD,
and he will sustain you;
he will never allow the righteous to be shaken.

PSALM 55:22 CSB

Although the rim of the mountain looked treacherous, if
the hikers followed the path and held onto the ropes, they
would be safe. They would, however, need to understand
and follow all of the rules. Most of the group were
committed to the leadership of the guide, who was an
expert climber. Ralph, however, liked to test the limits. He
made jokes about falling and purposefully loosened his
grip on the rope which allowed it to slacken for the two
hikers closest to him. At the first opportunity, the jokester
was removed from the climb and told he would never be
allowed back again.

We don't have righteousness on our own, but we're given it
in Christ. When we are tempted to sin, we can resist by the
power of the Holy Spirit, and then choose to be wise instead
of foolish. Place your feet upon the rock and you will never
be moved. He promised to carry us through the struggles
and to protect those whose hearts are fully his.

Grace upon Grace

Give your cares to Jesus, knowing you are eternally safe.

Our Struggles

"I dwell in the high and holy place, and also with him who is of a contrite and lowly spirit, to revive the spirit of the lowly, and to revive the heart of the contrite."

ISAIAH 57:15 ESV

Egan was disappointed at his failing grades. He had worked so hard as a college freshman, yet his GPA was suffering. He went to his counselor who proceeded to make an appointment with the president of the school. Egan was certain that he was being suspended, but instead the president sat down beside him. He said that in his first year of college, he was also suspended due to failing a few classes. He assured Egan that help would be provided and someday the boy could experience the same level of success that the president had enjoyed if he were willing to work hard.

While we are on this earth, we will battle sin. Like the apostle Paul, we do the very thing we don't want to do, seeing ourselves as wretched. Yet, we have a God who became man and understands our struggles. Jesus bows down to meet those who are remorseful. He forgives and renews them. Never hesitate to go to him who left his throne to save you.

Grace upon Grace

You can give Jesus your weary, sinful soul, knowing he will always redeem you.

Spent for His Glory

"Truly, truly I say to you, unless a grain of wheat falls into the earth and dies, it remains alone; but if it dies, it bears much fruit."

JOHN 12:24 NASB

Zoey hated seeing her friend change so much. There was a time they were like-minded, both wanting to do the will of the Lord. The new crowd that had attracted Hannah, though, was altering her attitude. When once Hannah had lived sacrificially, she now lived for the moment. She was always out buying expensive things and frequenting parties. Zoey was left behind but remained determined to continue with the plans that they had once created together. Zoey would go to the mission field alone. God blessed her beyond her imagination as her friend continued to fall away from the Lord's path.

When we live only for this world, we place ourselves in danger of forgoing the life God has planned for us. Time on this earth is short. How can we best spend our days furthering his kingdom? Someday we will account for how we lived and served Jesus.

Grace upon Grace

Strive to live a selfless life of serving others.

Heavenly Royalty

I am forgotten as though I were dead;
I have become like broken pottery.

PSALM 31:12 NIV

Many of us experience times when we feel deserted. Maybe we were offended by someone or became discouraged by life's difficulties and disappointments. We might start to listen to the lies from the enemy. He says we deserve the bad stuff, and that we aren't good enough. He tries to tell us that the fault lies solely with us. He whispers that we're unnecessary, that no one cares. The crack in our heart widens and our tears fall.

If we would simply look up and pray, we would recognize the presence of Jesus. He wants each of us to know the truth. We are chosen; we are treasured; we are loved; there is a good plan for our lives that was devised by the Creator of everything. We aren't common; we are heavenly royalty. The lies we hear are from the one who has already been defeated. We, on the other hand, are blessed beyond measure and adored by the one true God who tells us to call him Abba. Speak his words over yourself today for they are your truth.

Grace upon Grace

If you need a reminder of who you are in Christ, simply open God's Word.

Righteously Devoted

The LORD tests the righteous,
But the wicked and the one who loves violence
His soul hates.

PSALM 11:5 NKJV

The room was silent, but everyone could sense the tension. Those who passed the test would receive the accreditation to become surgeons and have the opportunity to save lives. When Everly was caught looking at Lorna's test, she was removed from the final and stripped of her chance to proceed. Anyone who cheated was not trustworthy enough for a patient to be placed into their hands. Allowing such a person to enter the field would be dangerous.

God allows his own, those he calls righteous, to be tested to see if they are upright and whether or not their allegiance to him remains regardless of their circumstances. If you are undergoing trials, put your trust in him alone, for he works the impossible on behalf of those who are righteously devoted to him.

Grace upon Grace

When you are tested, trust God is using it for his purpose.

Humble in Confession

Confess your sins to each other and pray for each other so that you may be healed. The earnest prayer of a righteous person has great power and produces wonderful results.

JAMES 5:16 NLT

The Bible study group was quiet as Victoria stepped forward to make a confession. She had abused a substance and was now suffering the physical consequences of her poor choice. Seeking forgiveness, Victoria asked if the power of prayer from those present could be enacted on her behalf. In humility and compassion, they all gathered around her and prayed, but it was the prayer of a shy member, Natalie, which touched them the most. Natalie rarely spoke, but she approached the throne of heaven with such power and eloquence that they knew God was right in the center of them.

There is power in prayer, especially when we appeal to God with humility, believing the Lord can accomplish anything. If you have something for which you need prayer support or a secret sin that you want to get off your chest, go to those you know to be righteous and trustworthy. Ask for prayer and go in faith, knowing that God will be with you.

Grace upon Grace

Confess any sin before you pray for others.

Joy in Jesus

A joyful heart is good medicine,
but a broken spirit dries up the bones.

PROVERBS 17:22 CSB

There was a distinct difference between the twins. Kinsley was optimistic, outgoing, and happy. Kellen was shy, quiet, and morose. Kinsley was healthy and did well in school while Kellen missed many days due to illness and fell behind in her studies. Try as the parents may, they couldn't influence their forlorn daughter to make lemonade out of lemons. They prayed and tried to intervene with positive reinforcement. They looked for any sign of Kellen taking a more uplifting outlook.

We have choices in life, the most important of which is over the issue of salvation. Accepting Christ as Savior opens the door to eternal joy, freedom, and deliverance from death. While on this earth, he offers abundant life that brings confidence in God's provisions. Without Jesus, there is no hope or opportunity for a life with meaning. If you know Christ, choose joy and be cheerful for your future is secure.

Grace upon Grace

Live a life that speaks of the joy you have in Jesus.

Rebuke all Fear

"Don't worry or surrender to your fear.
For you've believed in God,
now trust and believe in me also."

JOHN 14:1 TPT

Josie vowed that she would never watch another horror film, but her bestie, Maddie, always coerced her into watching something that freaked her out. Josie would try to sleep those nights but ended up waking her parents up with her nightmares and all the tossing and turning. They would make sure she was fully awake, then remind her that God tells us not to be afraid for he is our protector and defender.

The Word reminds us that our battle is against principalities and powers, not people, things, or situations. If we remember who our attacker is, we can rebuke him and his minions with Scripture. God's Word is truth. It is alive and will defeat the evil attempts of the enemy when we trust in what it says. There is no reason to be afraid for we have not been given a spirit of fear but of power, love, and a sound mind.

Grace upon Grace

Rebuke all fear and place your trust fully in the Lord.

The Great Commission

I do not account my life of any value nor as precious to myself, if only I may finish my course and the ministry that I received from the Lord Jesus, to testify to the gospel of the grace of God.

ACTS 20:24 ESV

There is but one goal we must complete. It was given to us by the one who created and saved us. It is a matter of life or death, spiritually speaking. After Jesus was resurrected, he left one directive for all of his disciples to fulfill: go and make more disciples.

Why do we ponder what God wants us to do with our lives? The Great Commission must be our target, regardless of what line of work we choose. Whether we are a nurse, a stay-at-home parent, a teacher, or anything else, Christ made it clear that our main objective is to make disciples.

Grace upon Grace

Don't hesitate; commit to carry out the calling God has given you.

One Truth

"Sanctify them in the truth;
Your word is truth."

JOHN 17:17 NASB

Preparing for her time to testify, Josephina absorbed every word the public defender said so that she wouldn't get tripped up. She knew he'd try to confuse her in hopes of making her say something to damage her testimony. Josephina was determined to speak accurately, honestly, and uprightly. When the lawyer for the accused was done, he realized that the account she gave had damaged his argument, proving his client guilty. She was justified by the truth she told.

Someday, all of humanity will stand before the throne of God. What will be your defense on that day? Were you a good person? That's great, but it will not suffice. All that will deliver you is the sacrifice of the Savior. There is no other name; there is no other truth; there's only Jesus. On that day when the accuser tries to take you down, if you are in Christ he will speak on your behalf. He will call you his very own, paid for by his blood.

Grace upon Grace

*Be reassured that through confession and forgiveness,
you are truly saved.*

Faithful Blessings

"I will make them and the places all around My hill a blessing; and I will cause showers to come down in their season; there shall be showers of blessing."

EZEKIEL 34:26 NKJV

A drought had caused the grass to turn brown, the dirt to crack, and the crops to fail. The little town, dependent on farming, was moving toward extinction. The townspeople gathered at the country church and Albert, known to walk with Jesus, called on everyone to fast and pray. Collectively, they worshiped, petitioned the Lord, and cried out for mercy on their land. The next day the sky turned gray, and the clouds burst open. A healing rain poured down from heaven. God was faithful and they celebrated by dancing in the rain.

When we humbly commit to fast and pray, the Father draws near and responds in his wisdom. We may receive the answer we hoped for or not. We must trust that he knows what is best for he is a perfect Father who loves to give good gifts to his children. Know that whatever he does, it is meant to bless you out of his abundant love.

Grace upon Grace

Spend a few moments praising the Lord for showering you with blessings.

Book of Life

You have come to the assembly of God's firstborn children, whose names are written in heaven. You have come to God himself, who is the judge over all things. You have come to the spirits of the righteous ones in heaven who have now been made perfect.

HEBREWS 12:23 NLT

Skylar had no siblings in town. In fact, all her relatives lived across the country. When Skylar was feeling her loneliest, a neighbor noticed and invited her to go to church. She wasn't a religious person, but she knew she needed to be with people. When she heard the truth of God's love, Christ's sacrifice, and the forgiveness of sins, Skylar went forward to ask the Savior into her heart.

In Christ, we have a massive family and a rich heritage. We're joint heirs with Christ and joined to the entire church, his body. When we are home in heaven, we will be able to sit and visit with our relations, Moses, Joshua, Esther, Ruth, and other great people of the faith. And we're counted amongst them with our names written in the Book of Life.

Grace upon Grace

Your family tree should include a line of the family of Christ.

Take It to Jesus

Cast all your anxiety on Him,
because He cares about you.

1 PETER 5:7 NASB

Sadie was a desolate woman. She bit her fingernails down so far that they started to bleed. Her anxiety was at fever pitch. Knowing, though, that she could go to Jesus at any hour, she bowed her head and cried out to him. Sadie loved his comfort but asked if he would please send someone to give her godly advice and to reassure her. There was a knock on the door, and she opened it to find a dear, compassionate friend. She knew God had answered her prayer and sent this woman to minister to her.

The best person we can take our concerns to is Jesus. He is always there to calm us, instruct us, and answer our prayers. He can even send us someone who will minister to us. If we place our faith in who he is and what he can do, we will find the help we desire. He loves us more than we can comprehend. He calls us to lay our problems at his feet so he can carry them for us.

Grace upon Grace

*Thank Jesus for giving you brothers and sisters in Christ
to care for you.*

Cleansing

Create in me a clean heart, O God,
and renew a right spirit within me.

PSALM 51:10 ESV

Quinn had faced temptation and given in. Now it was hard to even look at herself in the mirror. She had known better but had foolishly followed her whim to involve herself in something that went badly. Quinn was hard on herself; she felt as if there was no way to repair the damage she had done, and the devil was relentless with his attack of lies on her. But God cut right through the enemy's scheme and went straight to her heart. He whispered to Quinn that there was forgiveness and a fresh start.

There is nothing that can separate us from God if we recognize and repent of our sins. We will always be forgiven if turn to the only one who can save us. He loves restoring his children to himself, and he desires that we bring any sin to him so that he can wipe the slate clean. Once we speak our repentance, he removes all of our transgressions and never thinks of them again. Confess and enjoy the revival of your relationship with your heavenly Father.

Grace upon Grace

*After you confess your sin, receive your cleansing,
and be restored to the Father.*

We are Sinners

All have sinned and fall short of the glory of God.

ROMANS 3:23 NASB

Both Caroline and Gabriella needed scholarships, so this was a do-or-die situation. The big game would bring recruiters from the most important colleges. The girls sized up their biggest competition, then panicked. They knew they couldn't come up to the other team's level, so they plotted. Prior to the tournament Caroline and Gabriella would sneak into the locker room and sabotage their competitor's equipment just enough so no one would notice but it would result in a failure on the court. The coach entered the room as they were destroying the evidence and eliminated them from the event.

We're all sinners who fall far short of God's glory. If we are left to defend ourselves, we will be destined for destruction. Just like the two athletes, we'd resort to anything to gain entrance to heaven, but we would fail miserably. We can't work our way there and we can't talk our way in. All we can do is surrender our lives to Jesus and be assured that we will live eternally.

Grace upon Grace

Jesus provided salvation for everyone including you!

His Strength

My flesh and my heart may fail,
but God is the strength of my heart
and my portion forever.

PSALM 73:26 NIV

The news made Jade weak at the knees and she felt as though she couldn't catch her breath. She'd just had lunch with her friend yesterday and would never have believed it would be the last time she would see her. The brevity of life hit her like a ton of bricks. Jade cried out to God for those who had been left behind—a wonderful husband and two small children. She asked him for strength amid the sorrow, to bring comfort and assistance to the suffering family and friends.

We cannot predict what a day may bring. Unexpected events, especially traumatic ones, can alter our lives for the rest of our days. God wants to hold our failing hearts and show us the path forward. He will support us in our distress and provide what we need, whether it is physical, emotional, or spiritual. He will also give us the power to minister to the ones closest to a tragedy. He has promised to be faithful to us and empower us in our moment of need if we request it from him.

Grace upon Grace

Strengthen someone with God's Word to lift them up.

Rest

> "Come to Me, all you who labor and are heavy laden,
> and I will give you rest."
>
> MATTHEW 11:28 NKJV

The weary office cleaner applied thick lotion to her dry
and cracking skin. Cora had scrubbed with excellence
every inch of the spaces she was hired to clean, faithfully
performing her work as unto God. She believed she was
doing a great service to others even though some looked at
her duties as beneath them. Cora noticed in some offices
that workers would surf the web for personal reasons
during their work hours, and she wondered how they could
cheat their employers. At night, she was bone tired but
experienced sweet rest from the Lord, knowing she had
pleased him with the integrity of her work.

If you are a hard, honest laborer, you know the respite of
a solid night's sleep when you are exhausted. Whether it is
from mental or physical endeavors, God blesses those who
perform their tasks as if they were doing it solely for him.

Grace upon Grace

*Be thankful for the work you have
and the restorative sleep God grants you.*

Sin Spreads

When Adam sinned, sin entered the world.
Adam's sin brought death, so death spread to everyone,
for everyone sinned.

ROMANS 5:12 NLT

Arianna lingered at the window watching the other neighborhood kids play and knowing she couldn't go outside. She was contagious with the chicken pox, but she desperately wanted to join the others in the warm sun. It would help her forget how badly she itched! While her mom was resting, Arianna snuck out and romped with all the children. The other moms, realizing what the marks were on the girl, gasped and quickly scurried their young ones home. Everyone there caught the disease, and Arianna was in trouble for carelessly giving it to her friends.

When Adam and Eve made the fateful decision to eat from the Tree of Knowledge of Good and Evil, the sin that resulted spread to all of humanity. Death was the punishment for the family of man. When you feel the compulsion to blame the first couple, realize that if we'd been them, we'd probably had taken that bite ourselves. The disease of our trespasses has a cure, and his name is Jesus.

Grace upon Grace

*Death is a part of life, but due to grace from Christ's death,
you have eternal life.*

Be Bold

> "I have told you these things so that in me you may have peace. You will have suffering in this world. Be courageous! I have conquered the world."
>
> JOHN 16:33 CSB

"Jesus freak!" The group of kids yelled at Lydia, the tenth-grade girl. She shared her testimony with her home room that morning and the other kid were not appreciative. In fact, they were downright mean. Lydia started to question if she did the right thing by telling them all about Jesus and what he means to her. Then she remembered her pastor saying that we should rejoice when we are mocked for our faith. In suffering for Jesus this way, we are aligning ourselves with him. If we are unashamed of him, he will be unashamed of us. He will present us to his Father as his own.

It is hard to be rejected for our beliefs. Being fearful of what people may say can cause us to be silent. Wouldn't you rather lose the world and gain eternity with God? Don't be quiet; share the gospel and help others know Jesus. Be courageous for through Christ, you have already won the victory.

Grace upon Grace

Be bold in sharing about Christ and rejoice in the persecution.

Close to Jesus

"I am the vine; you are the branches. Whoever abides in me and I in him, he it is that bears much fruit, for apart from me you can do nothing."

JOHN 15:5 ESV

When an infant is born there is complete dependency on his parents. The child has no means of caring for himself but must have the moment-to-moment assistance of mom and dad. The little one cries out for the closeness and comfort of his parents, instinctively knowing that that is where his needs will be met. Without the help and constant aid of the adults, the baby could not survive.

As a child of God, we have been given spiritual gifts and the power of the Holy Spirit. Yet if we do not remain close to Jesus, we will accomplish nothing. Trying to do the will of God through human effort always has failure written on it. He's our lifeblood and since he is the vine, we, the branches, receive our sustenance from him. If we remain humble and understand that without him, we can do nothing, he will work in mighty ways to multiply the fruit in our lives. He has given us authority and power, but it can only be manifested through a life surrendered and submitted to Jesus.

Grace upon Grace

Remain humbly close to Jesus, for only through him will your life produce eternal fruit.

He has Overcome

The afflictions of the righteous are many,
But the LORD rescues him from them all.

PSALM 34:19 NASB

Many people in the church looked at the Bradner family
as if they were cursed. As soon as one problem in their
lives was resolved, another assailed them. No one could
understand how they could be so peaceful and rebound the
way they did. Then one morning in church, the Bradners
shared the secret. How could they be downhearted
when God was so faithful? Even though new trials
kept happening, he always rescued them from every
hardship. They knew from experience that whatever they
encountered, their God would always be their deliverer and
for that, they rejoiced.

We've been forewarned so there should be no surprises—
we will suffer while on earth. But take heart! Jesus has
promised to defend us, and one day when he returns, he
will wipe our tears away. The battle will end and through
Christ, we win!

Grace upon Grace

*Take heart, the score with sin was settled
when Christ won the victory!*

Transformation

If anyone is in Christ, the new creation has come:
The old has gone, the new is here!

2 CORINTHIANS 5:17 NIV

The new science project for the students was to watch the process of a caterpillar becoming a butterfly. They tracked each step of its metamorphosis. When the caterpillar stopped eating, it hung itself from a small branch or twig. Then it began the busy work of spinning a velvety cocoon. Inside this cocoon a transformation was taking place, and the result was the emergence of a beautiful butterfly. The former appearance of the bug was no more, for a new creature exited the chrysalis and its beauty was admired by all the students.

When an unbeliever is transformed into a Christ follower, old sinful patterns start to fall away, and new convictions appear. The believer no longer lusts after a worldly lifestyle but longs to please their Savior. Desires for certain pastimes no longer lure them. There is a distinct difference between the old and the new. This is how many come to Jesus—by watching the testimony of a life renewed.

Grace upon Grace

*Live such a transformed life that others
can tell that Christ lives in you.*

September

The LORD is compassionate
and gracious,
slow to anger,
abounding in love.

PSALM 103:8 NIV

New Creations

"Behold, I will do a new thing,
Now it shall spring forth;
Shall you not know it?"

ISAIAH 43:19 NKJV

Olivia awoke on her wedding morning realizing that today, the course of her life would change. It was the day she would join her life to Anthony's, becoming marriage partners with the person she had dreamed of from the time she was a young girl. Two families would be connected through this marriage and with this union came the hope of new family members through the blessing of children. Olivia would have a new name and a new bright future, and she had God to thank for it.

Jesus changed everything when he died on the cross and was resurrected. Sin and death were destroyed. Those who receive him are no longer the same but are transformed. Just like roads in the wilderness and rivers in the desert, Jesus made a way down a narrow path for us to be a completely new creation in him.

Grace upon Grace

You are a sinner saved by grace and a new creation through the power of the cross.

Be Like Jesus

Love one another deeply as brothers and sisters.
Take the lead in honoring one another.

ROMANS 12:10 CSB

It had been a long day wrought with annoyances that piled up like a week's worth of garbage. A careless word spoken by a family member, traffic that was jammed at the most inconvenient time, and dirt tracked across the newly scrubbed floor by the family dog. A rushed morning stole away the time normally spent in Scripture and prayer. Stella's spirit was not prepared for a day of trials, and her attitude showed it. She found herself short tempered, offended by everyone, and picking an unprovoked fight with her friend.

God knows our sin nature and how easily we can give into temptation if we are not seeking him through the study of the Word, worship, and prayer. We get stressed, saying harsh things we normally wouldn't. We spew angry insults out of our irritation. Offenses are blown out of proportion. God has given us a better way. Stop, pray, and confess. Be kind, patient, forgiving, and loving, in other words, be like Jesus.

Grace upon Grace

Start every day with Jesus and get filled with his Spirit.

Esteem

> "House of Israel, can I not treat you as this potter treats his clay?"—this is the LORD's declaration. "Just like clay in the potter's hand, so are you in my hand, house of Israel."
>
> JEREMIAH 18:6 CSB

A crowd had gathered to watch through the window of the art center. Students were focused on molding their creations with stoneware clay. There were bowls, pitchers, and vases. Dillan used earthenware clay to form a bust of a woman's head. He'd get just so far, frown, then crush the clay into a blob. He'd begin again only to end up destroying it again. Dillan worked for weeks until he finally completed something he was pleased with.

Our Father, the one true God, is the one who allows us each to breathe every morning. He is the Creator of all, and the final say on everything. We are the work of his hands, made to reflect his image. If we grasped the power of all that he is and fearfully respected him as we should, we would submit, faces to the ground, humbled to even approach him. Do we give God the esteem that is due?

Grace upon Grace

Trust in God's great love to do with you as he wills.

He Hears Us

Out of the depths I cry to you, O LORD!
O Lord, hear my voice!
Let your ears be attentive to the voice of my pleas for mercy!

PSALM 130:1–2 ESV

When Everlee was babysitting, she ran to her car to retrieve something. That naughty little boy, Raymond, locked her out of the house in the pouring rain. She begged him to let her in, explaining that if he did, she would forgive and forget. She even offered ice cream as a reward, but Raymond wouldn't budge. Realizing she had put her phone in her pocket earlier, Everlee called his parents. Although they were an hour away, they promised to get home as soon as possible. The next time Raymond's parents asked her to watch their son Everlee quickly refused.

Whenever we call out to God, he is attentive to our cries. There may be times when the rescue doesn't come immediately, but if we have faith, we know that he has heard us and is working on our behalf. Whether petitioning him for forgiveness, a need, or on behalf of another, he will have the answer in his great mercy.

Grace upon Grace

You can call out to the Lord any time of the day or night,
and he will hear your prayers and answer them.

Making Disciples

"Go, therefore, and make disciples of all the nations,
baptizing them in the name of the Father and the Son
and the Holy Spirit, teaching them to follow all that I
commanded you; and behold, I am with you always,
to the end of the age."

MATTHEW 28: 19-20 NASB

The instructions were clear and precise. The trainees were
told where they should go, to whom they should go, and
how they are to do the job with excellence. The trainees
were assured that they could always contact their superior if
they had questions. Mr. Phipps would be ready at any hour
to assist them and provide any knowledge they would need
to complete their work. There really was no excuse not to
complete the job with which they were entrusted.

There's only one Great Commission: we are to go and make
disciples of all people. Why do we struggle with this? If
we are uneasy or concerned about man's opinion, we need
to confess that. Jesus promises to be with us, so we have
nothing to fear. Making disciples isn't a request; it's his
command.

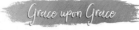

Grace upon Grace

*Don't shrink back from speaking Jesus' name
and sharing the gospel with the world.*

Patient in Affliction

Be joyful in hope, patient in affliction, faithful in prayer.

ROMANS 12:12 NIV

The dental work was overdue. The day had come for the oral surgery. The doctor said that the third day of Anjelica's recovery would be the hardest. Sure enough, day three arrived with a vengeance. She read her Bible for comfort, finding that she could confidently hold onto the hope of this difficult experience passing. Anjelica just needed to be patient through the pain and to pray through this day in faith. As she concentrated on these things, she felt a sense of joy rise in her. She praised God for his faithfulness to stay by her side, and the knowledge that he would heal her in his time.

Pain is hard to live through and often debilitating at the time. If anyone understands physical pain, it is our Savior. During those times when we are suffering in our body we can go to him, and he will comfort us. He understands trauma that is beyond our comprehension. He knows the joy that comes afterward, for what he endured brought our healing and salvation.

Grace upon Grace

Jesus is your healing when you're hurt and your hope when you experience pain.

Never Forsaken

The LORD will perfect that which concerns me;
Your mercy, O LORD, endures forever;
Do not forsake the works of Your hands.

PSALM 138:8 NKJV

Peyton offered to make all the costumes for the school play. The process went from pleasant to stressful when the work became more time-consuming than she had anticipated. It was even more complicated because the material arrived late, people kept missing their fittings, and the organizers changed the completion date for the costumes to an earlier time. Peyton prayed, asking God for mercy in bringing someone to help her. She asked in faith and kept working while she waited. Not only did one other mom step up, but three called by the end of that very day, asking how they could help.

Nothing is too insignificant for us to carry to his throne. If he is interested enough to number our hairs, don't you think he cares about everything that concerns us? He can fix any situation. Trust that he'll be there when you need him, offering mercy in times of distress.

Grace upon Grace

In your time of need, ask for God's merciful comfort.

God's Handiwork

"I knew you before I formed you in your mother's womb. Before you were born I set you apart and appointed you as my prophet to the nations."

JEREMIAH 1:5 NLT

The high school science project required the students to construct a model of an invisible man. Every organ and vessel were to be visible. It boggled the minds of the students to see the intricacies of the human body. The kids who had been taught that man had just evolved were now having doubts. A debate ensued which gave a young Christian, Rubena, a great opportunity to stand before the class and share. She told them they were God's handiwork, and that he supervised every aspect of their development in the womb. She assured them it was his breath that gave them life.

Conception to development to birth—it is all miraculous. Along with forming every part of the complex human system, God designs our personalities. He plans his purpose for our lives and sets us apart to do his divine will. The God of the universe personally made you. Isn't it wonderful beyond comprehension?

Grace upon Grace

Be amazed that God was there designing you in your mother's womb, and he sees you now.

Preparation

I call to God Most High,
to God who fulfills his purpose for me.

PSALM 57:2 CSB

Jennie couldn't understand the constant need to practice her violin. Her parents insisted she continue. They assured her that someday she would thank them. Calluses developed on her fingers, and she cried, saying she wanted to stop. Nevertheless, Jennie was not allowed to quit. Years later when she auditioned for a school known for producing the best in the performing arts, she stood on the stage with confidence. Jennie played her violin to perfection and was grateful for her parents' encouragement.

Trials can bring bitter tears and discouragement in the moment. Sometimes we only see what is happening in the moment, and we can't imagine how it may benefit us in the years to come. In those times we need to remember who designed our future. He allows occurrences which mature us and make us stronger. We can be assured that he will equip us properly.

Grace upon Grace

Call on God, and he will equip you for his purpose.

Healthy Fear

Blessed is everyone who fears the LORD,
who walks in his ways!

PSALM 128:1 ESV

Whenever Phil Leland entered the room, you could hear a pin drop. Everyone stood at attention. He was a respected national champion in the art of karate. Knowing he could break a brick with his bare hands created a healthy fear. The young students memorized the tenets of the craft and followed the instructions exactly. They executed every move as he directed. The students watched him and studied him, wanting to represent their school well. Most of all, they wanted to please their teacher with their efforts.

When we have an intimate relationship with the Lord, we learn to understand his character and power. We learn the kind of respect that is defined in the Bible as fear. We are in awe of what he can do, acknowledging the fact that we are only alive because he ordained it. It doesn't mean we are frightened of him; it means we hold him in the highest regard.

Grace upon Grace

Give God respect, humility, and submission for his glory.

God First

"Seek his kingdom,
and these things will be provided for you."

LUKE 12:31 CSB

Whenever Valentina passed the magazine section in the store it was as if it was calling her name. From beauty tips to consumer products, they all lured her, creating a lust for those possessions. Lately she also noticed that she became anxious and wanted to earn more so she could have more. Depression played with her mind as Valentina was unable to purchase all that she thought she needed. She noticed her thoughts were mainly on herself, and she started to realize that she needed to readjust her priorities.

Scripture assures us that we never need to worry about our provisions because Jesus is our perfect provider. Joy floods our souls when we can bring blessings to those who lack the things we can provide. Peace fills our minds when we determine to serve others and not place ourselves as number one. All we could ever need follows. God's righteousness, his approval, and his good gifts come to those who put his kingdom above everything else.

Grace upon Grace

*Put God's kingdom and the needs of others above your own,
and he will provide everything you need.*

Preparation

We are God's handiwork, created in Christ Jesus to do good
works, which God prepared in advance for us to do.

EPHESIANS 2:10 NIV

Bella and Robert were so excited about their upcoming
birth. As a first-time mom, Bella spent hours knitting,
decorating the baby's room, and reading books. Knowing
they were having a boy, Robert pulled out his old baseball
mitt and daydreamed about how he would toss the ball with
his son. Most importantly, they discussed how they wanted
to raise their child in the ways of the Lord. They prayed
over their baby, hoping he would pursue the purpose for
which God created him.

Consider the meaning of *handiwork*. It means to be created
by the maker's hands. We were formed by God. He decided
our path in advance. Do you marvel that he planned your
life individually and specifically? If we fully comprehended
this, would we listen for his leading more intently? Would
we obey more quickly? Consider the truth of how special
you are to God. Seek the purpose which he determined for
you before you even took your first breath.

Grace upon Grace

As you thank God for his handiwork in your life, be specific.

He's Coming Back

The vision is yet for an appointed time;
But at the end it will speak, and it will not lie.
Though it tarries, wait for it;
Because it will surely come,
It will not tarry.

HABAKKUK 2:3 NKJV

The dream Leena had about her beloved, Matthew, was so vivid that when she awoke, she expected to see him. Leena even felt all the emotions that came like the bursting of a dam. Matthew walked into the terminal wearing the uniform that had worn on the day he left. He had served his country with honor, always assuring her he would be back one day to spend the rest of his life with her. When Leena realized it was just a dream, the longing in her heart surged, for she desperately desired Matthew's return.

Prophets spoke of the return of Christ. Are we prepared like the virgins who made sure their lamps were filled with oil, or are we preoccupied with other things? Do we long to see him and be with him, or are we entrenched in this world? He's coming back, and it could be today! Are you ready?

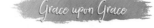

Grace upon Grace

Live as if Christ will return today.

Lean on God

On the day I called, you answered me;
you increased my strength within me.

PSALM 138:3 CSB

Ivan had always been healthy, and in fact many people
commented on how he never got sick. As his age increased,
though, he started experiencing little aches. He ignored
them, pushing himself just as hard as he had in his
younger years. Then one day, Ivan couldn't push anymore.
He realized that possibly he was in worse shape than he
originally thought. He prayed and felt led to see a doctor. A
disease was diagnosed, but he knew his spirit was healthy
for he had committed his heart to Jesus years ago and
always leaned on God's strength.

Time marches on, and regardless of how great we may feel
today, physical changes will come. Isn't it reassuring to
know that we can continue to grow stronger and healthier
in our spiritual lives? There's no limitation to becoming
more like Jesus because his goodness and grace is infinite.
Regardless of what we may face in this earthly body, God is
our portion without end.

Grace upon Grace

*As you age, make sure you keep maturing
in your walk with the Lord.*

Caring Encouragement

You, dear friends, must build each other up in your most holy faith, pray in the power of the Holy Spirit.

JUDE 20 NLT

When Savannah opened her heart to the people in her small group and confessed her troubles, there was no end to their support. She talked about how she was dealing with her sins, and immediately they went to her side, laid hands on her, and prayed. There was no judgment in their words; they only gave encouragement and the acknowledgement of how God would be faithful to provide what she needed. The experience of this support gave Savannah peace. The presence of the Holy Spirit was palpable as the body worked together, beautifully upholding their sister in the faith.

There is never a good reason for stepping away from another Christ follower in their time of need. We are all at some point going to encounter a difficulty or engage in sin that we later need to confess. When our Christian sisters have our backs, it brings healing. We should always offer our prayers, our time, and our resources. We are a spiritual family, birthed through the blood of Jesus. We are meant to walk in loving deference to one another.

Grace upon Grace

Be the voice of caring encouragement
and graciously serve the body of Christ.

Testify

Do not be ashamed of the testimony about our Lord,
nor of me his prisoner, but share in suffering for the gospel
by the power of God.

2 TIMOTHY 1:8 ESV

Because Aubrey was afraid of cancel culture, she thought
long and hard about how she would handle the imminent
conversation. She was certain that her associates felt
differently than she did and would be vocally adamant.
Aubrey was concerned for her job and the friendships she
developed at work. She also knew she couldn't just dismiss
the truth to which she was committed. The question was
whether she was ready to suffer the loss of her career and
the relationships with those people she cared deeply about
in order to stay true to her beliefs.

Scripture says if we're ashamed of Jesus, he will be ashamed
of us. That thought is like a knife to the heart. After all
he has done for us, shouldn't we be willing to relinquish
anything to speak of his cross? If we love Jesus, we will be
compelled to testify to the truth of his saving grace.

Grace upon Grace

*Be devoted to telling the good news,
empowered by Christ.*

Misguided

Many plans are in a person's heart,
But the advice of the LORD will stand.

PROVERBS 19:21 NASB

The plan that Brooklyn had concocted made sense in her own mind. When she composed it in an online personal document she was impressed with her own genius. It didn't matter to her that she hadn't sought any counsel from the other leaders because she already knew that she didn't need anyone else's opinion. Brooklyn didn't even pray about it because it made total sense that God would approve. After all, she would be doing work for his kingdom, so why would there be any other plan to consider?

We can jump ahead of God when we mistakenly think something is his will just because it is ministry. He determines the work we are to do even before we are born. If we don't follow his lead, we may be trying to step into something designed for someone else. We should consult Scripture, wise godly counsel, and prayer. If we don't first seek his purpose for us, we are not likely in his will. It is the Lord's master design for us that will succeed.

Grace upon Grace

Be careful not to foolishly move ahead of God out of excitement or pride.

Requirements

He has shown you, O man, what is good;
And what does the LORD require of you
But to do justly,
To love mercy,
And to walk humbly with your God?

MICAH 6:8 NKJV

The Bible study group was given homework. They were to determine what verse spoke about God's requirement for all believers. Many answered to obey the Ten Commandments, some said it was to be saved by the blood of Christ. Both are true, but what is required was in the wording of the assignment. The result is found in Micah 6:8. We are to act justly and to love mercy. The third requirement is to walk humbly with the Lord. Humility is prized and honored in the eyes of God.

Justice means being fair and seeking to uphold the truth. Loving mercy means to show compassion, be forgiving, and bearing consequences for another just as Jesus did in when he paid for our sins on the cross. Humility means not to consider yourselves better than others, knowing your identity and value in Christ. Walk with God in this manner.

Grace upon Grace

*Live the requirements of Micah 6:8
through the Holy Spirit's power.*

Consequences

"Get up, for it is your duty to tell us how to proceed in
setting things straight. We are behind you,
so be strong and take action."

 EZRA 10:4 NLT

When the group decided that the thrill of pushing the
envelope was more compelling than the legal decrees,
they defiled themselves. The law was unmistakable in its
demands. Any veering from the mandate would carry strict
consequences. It was a matter of time before they would
have to decide. Would they do whatever was required to set
things straight?

Israel ignored God's laws about marrying women from
foreign nations. Once the Israelites were confronted by
the prophet Ezra, however, they had to choose. They could
repent and separate from those wives and children, or they
could no longer remain within Israel. Losing their families
was a hefty price but most of them were willing to pay. So,
they repented. When we are aware of God's way for us and
yet choose to sin, there are always consequences. Study his
Word so that you can be obedient and receive his blessings.

Grace upon Grace

Value God's approval far above choosing your own way.

Purity

Don't you know that your body is a temple of the Holy
Spirit who is in you, whom you have from God?
You are not your own.

1 CORINTHIANS 6:19 CSB

Delilah and Kimberley were relentlessly inquiring about
Autumn's love life. They told her times had changed and that
even kids in the church were being intimate nowadays. If
Autumn hadn't yet, she should sleep with her boyfriend. In
her heart, Autumn knew she would wait for marriage; she
believed it was a sin against God to engage beforehand. His
moral law was no different now than when it was written.
She knew that Jesus paid a great price to redeem her, so she
decided she would stay pure in her body and her mind.

Culture wants to convince us that God's standards in his
Word are outdated. Scripture has not changed. The truth
is, we were paid for in full. If you accepted Jesus as your
Savior, then you belong entirely to him. We are his temple
indwelled by his Holy Spirit. Why would we ever willingly
carry his Spirit into an act of sin? Don't let others deceive
you—our goal must always be to glorify him in our bodies
and with our actions, our speech, and our thoughts.

Grace upon Grace

*Seek purity and recommit your body, words, actions,
and thoughts to glorify God.*

Weak Strength

For the sake of Christ, then, I am content with weaknesses,
insults, hardships, persecutions, and calamities.
For when I am weak, then I am strong.

2 CORINTHIANS 12:10 ESV

The world applauds and idolizes those who are physically
strong. We are fans of professional sports figures, and we
don't even balk at the exorbitant salaries they earn. We are
voracious about our runs and our workouts. We look at
those who do not labor to improve their strength as lazy
or weak. But what about those who lack strength or have a
disability? Are they pitied or appreciated for their special
God-given gifts and talents?

Some of the most gifted people, those who have had the
greatest influence on God's kingdom, are those whom
many would see as non-candidates for the spread of the
gospel. Consider Joni Eareckson Tada, a quadriplegic; Nick
Vujicic, a man with no arms or legs; and a young Christian
actor with Down Syndrome, David DeSanctis. When we
acknowledge our inabilities and weaknesses to God, that is
when he can do miracles through us.

Grace upon Grace

Recognize your weaknesses and ask God to work through
you with his strengths.

No Time Like Today

Teach us to number our days,
That we may present to You a heart of wisdom.

PSALM 90:12 NASB

As Lillian approached a landmark birthday, she looked in the mirror and wondered how she could feel so young yet look so old. It caused her to review her life. What had she really accomplished? There were the average things and admittedly many blessings, but what mark would she leave on this world once she was gone? It lit a fire under her, and Lillian began to pray. She asked God for wisdom to discern how to sacrificially live the rest of her life for the purpose he created her for.

When you take an account of how life flies by, it's shocking. Scripture encourages us to number our days. You can get to a point when you realize time is slipping away and you may not have a long time to make the impact you had wanted to. Who are you praying for to come to Christ? Have you shared the gospel with them yet? There is no time like today, for no one knows what tomorrow will bring. Live your life for Jesus to the fullest, making the most of the time he has granted you.

Grace upon Grace

Be aware of your days so you can live them fully for Christ.

Spiritual Illumination

Your word is a lamp for my feet,
a light on my path.

PSALM 119:105 NIV

The campers stayed out hiking too long and now the sun was disappearing. They knew their way well but unfortunately Eddie and Fern got separated from the group. Neither Eddie nor Fern had taken a light, thinking they could share with the other people who were better prepared. Realizing their missing friends would not survive the cold night, the campers determined to search for them. As they moved, they shone their flashlights into the expanse and called their names. Soon, two voices cried out. Relieved and rescued, they all were grateful for their flashlights.

We move forward with an enlightened path if we commit ourselves to the study of God's Word. We don't need to wonder how we should live, or what he requires of us if we are students of the Bible. We can fight the powers of darkness and defeat the enemy using Scripture's battle plan. Our lives have the spiritual radiance of God's leading and his wisdom if we continually use his Word to train and guide us.

Grace upon Grace

Crave God's Word with the protection and guidance it brings.

Living Word

So shall My word be that goes forth from My mouth;
It shall not return to Me void,
But it shall accomplish what I please,
And it shall prosper in the thing for which I sent it.

ISAIAH 55:11 NKJV

Dean questioned the validity of the news his father shared at the table. Was the source reliable? The voices in culture were so divided that the young man's trust of the government had been shaken. Would the politician who made the statement need to retract it? What type of damage would it do in the meanwhile? Would it even accomplish good if it were true? Dean's father applauded him for questioning and encouraged him to seek discernment about the reports he would read.

Be judicious about what you hear and read. The Bible is infallible. It is the only book that is the breathing, living Word of God. It is alive and nothing else written can claim that. It is the Lord's truth to us, and it will always accomplish what it says. Trust what God has spoken. You may stake your life on it for all that it says will be fulfilled.

Grace upon Grace

Develop a love for the truth of God's Word so that you follow it closely all the days of your life.

He Holds the Future

"Only I can tell you the future before it even happens.
Everything I plan will come to pass for I do whatever I wish."

ISAIAH 46:10 NLT

The county fair arrived complete with clowns, Ferris wheels and cotton candy. Linda's family couldn't wait to experience the rides and the food unique to the event. Headed to the merry-go-round, they passed a woman dressed as a gypsy. She approached them, inviting them to her booth so she could read tea leaves that would reveal their future. They politely declined, telling her why they would not be joining her. They shared their faith in Christ relaying that his plan for their life was the only one they trusted in.

The only one who can declare the future is God. When he speaks in his Word, prophesying what will come, you can be certain of its fulfillment. Don't just take anyone's word who claims to have heard from God. Search his Scriptures to discern the truth. Pray and listen for his Spirit to guide you, so you can follow the path he designed specifically for you.

Grace upon Grace

*Be grateful that everything about today
and your future is in God's loving hands.*

Creator of All

Then God said, "Let us make man in our image, according to our likeness. They will rule the fish of the sea, the birds of the sky, the livestock, the whole earth, and the creatures that crawl on the earth."

GENESIS 1:26 CSB

Science is not exact. Some say science is the process of venturing a guess and then concocting investigations to try to prove those guesses. Others defend it by saying it is backed by prior discoveries, basic research, and rationale that covers all three main areas of earth, physical, and life sciences. There have been attempts at creating human life. There was success in the constructing of a single cell organism, but it malfunctioned when it was dividing, so no growth.

God spoke and life began. He breathed into the lungs of man and that breath became continuous. He gave his creation intellect, authority, and the imprint of himself. He didn't have to study, experiment, or repeat the process until he got it right. He just said the Word and it was done. Man will never be able to duplicate what only originates with our Lord. He will always be the only author of life.

Grace upon Grace

Think of the complexity of everything that exists by one architect—God!

Solely for His Purpose

"Whoever would save his life will lose it,
but whoever loses his life for my sake will find it."

MATTHEW 16:25 ESV

Alex bragged about his unproven courage. He said that his desire was to be a great protector. He repeatedly told people that if the situation ever arose when someone must step up to be the hero, he would be the first to volunteer. In secret, Alex hoped that day would never come. But it did; when it did, it surprised everyone who was aware of his moxie. Not only did Alex cower in the presence of danger, but he pulled someone else in front to be his human shield.

We are told in Scripture that when it comes to being a Christ follower, the way to save your life is to lose it. That means a believer must have a relentless drive to put Christ first. Our lives are no longer our priority. Whatever he calls us to, we must do. That will bring greater joy and an eternal impact that would never happen if we lived for ourselves.

Grace upon Grace

Allow God to be glorified by offering him every part of your life.

Peace and Confidence

"These things I have spoken to you so that in Me you may have peace. In the world you have tribulation, but take courage; I have overcome the world."

JOHN 16:33 NASB

There will be wars and rumors of wars. Family members will turn on one another and sin will be rampant. Nations will fight against one another with the desire to rule over each other. This is not a plot for a new movie; it is prophesied in Scripture. With the way our world is looking, many think the end is not far off. Jesus didn't want us to be caught off guard, so he warned us. Even if we are assailed by those who believe Christians are unloving and self-righteous, he wants us to remember that he has already won the battle.

Regardless of what storms may come, what speech may be silenced, or how our beliefs may be attacked, we have victory because of Jesus. We can have peace and courage. As Christ followers, our position in him is secure. So be at rest and trust. Be alert to the fact that regardless of our experiences in this life, he holds our future.

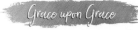

Grace upon Grace

Rest in the peace Jesus gives because of his victory and grace.

Nothing But Truth

All Scripture is God-breathed and is useful for teaching,
rebuking, correcting, and training in righteousness.

2 TIMOTHY 3:16 NIV

To be one of a small number of scholars to sit under the
genius of this awe-inspiring theologian was the opportunity
of a lifetime. He was considered one of the most brilliant
academics in his field. He who had only tutored a handful
of students in his lifetime, and the honor of learning from
him was extremely rare. It was an educational plethora of
information and those in attendance would find themselves
held in higher esteem for having learned from the master.

Intellectuals can teach us much about a myriad of subjects,
but only one course of study can instruct us to the point
of having eternal results. Every letter of Scripture has life
flowing through it. The Word can jump off the page and
into our souls, causing the heart to be given over to the
one who created it. The Word offers protection from the
danger of sin which leads to death. It tells of a love so great
that it defied the grave. It brings righteousness to those
who receive the Savior. God's Word is the ultimate teacher,
speaking nothing but truth.

Grace upon Grace

Thank God for his living Word that has led you to life.

Our Maker

"Everyone who is called by My name,
Whom I have created for My glory;
I have formed him, yes, I have made him."

ISAIAH 43:7 NKJV

The impending birth of Claire and Brent's first child was met with such anticipation they could hardly think of anything else. They chose to not find out the baby's gender ahead of time. But which of them would their offspring look like? Would he/she have blonde hair like mom or dark hair like dad? Will Claire and Brent be gazing into blue eyes or brown ones? Would it be a compliant child or a mischievous one? Most of all, would it follow the God of his or her parents, for that was what mattered the most.

God took the ultimate care in forming each person ever born. We were created for his purposes and his pleasure, yet to also be loved by him with the most lavish affection. He desires to be intimate with his children. What a glorious thing to be made by him and to belong to him!

Grace upon Grace

*Praise the God of the universe for the greatest love
you will ever know.*

October

The LORD is waiting
to show you mercy,
and is rising up
to show you compassion,
for the LORD is a just God.
All who wait patiently
for him are happy.

ISAIAH 30:18 CSB

God's Plan

For everything there is a season,
a time for every activity under heaven.

ECCLESIASTES 3:1 NLT

Now that Amberly had turned eighteen, she was thrilled for every upcoming season in her life. Where would a college degree take her? Whom might she marry? What would life look like ten or twenty years from now? Amberly planned and set goals so she could achieve her dreams—until she met the Savior. Then the wise young woman relinquished all of her hopes and dreams to the one who would surpass them all through his great and perfect purpose for her.

We have grandiose ideas and dreams for our lives. God's plan is best, and it's filled with a variety of realities. Ecclesiastes 3:1-8 says there are specific times for life events and different emotions, which often overtake the path in life. There's a time for birth, and a time to go home to God. There are times of weeping and times of dancing. History has shown a time for war and a time for peace. It is certain that life will have diverse experiences. One thing is more certain: when we invite Jesus into every moment, he will never leave us.

Grace upon Grace

*Express your need to have Jesus by your side
every minute of the day.*

Experience New Birth

If anyone is in Christ, he is a new creation;
the old has passed away, and see, the new has come!

2 CORINTHIANS 5:17 CSB

Sandra knew she was falling down a deep hole and had lost control over her life. She succumbed to things that even surprised her; she did things that made her feel guilty. With a minute amount of optimism, she looked for ways to dig herself out of the hole. She read philosophy and self-help books. Nothing seemed to fit. In desperation, she picked up a Bible. As Sandra read of the steadfast and sacrificial love, of the forgiveness and unconditional acceptance, it invigorated her heart. This was the answer—Jesus. All desire for past behavior dissipated as she experienced a new birth as a child of God.

When we give our lives over to Jesus, we become new creatures. He indwells us with his Holy Spirit. He beckons us to spend time with him. He transforms us to be like Christ, enabling us to bear fruit which will be evident for all eternity. Don't hesitate to experience his forgiveness and redemption, or the metamorphosis of a new life in Christ.

Grace upon Grace

You are continually being transformed through Christ's sacrifice on the cross.

Bestowed Royalty

You are a chosen people, a royal priesthood, a holy nation, a people for God's own possession, so that you may proclaim the excellencies of Him who has called you out of darkness into His marvelous light.

1 PETER 2:9 NASB

Little Elanna believed she was a princess. She would confidently proclaim it to anyone she met. Her mama encouraged her to be humble and not introduce herself as "Princess Elanna." The title felt so real to her though. Her Sunday school teacher had spoken of how we are God's own adopted children and that made us royal. That truth made the little girl's heart soar. She was a daughter of the most-high King.

We were lost but now we are found. We were dust and now we are treasured by the Lord most high. We're joint heirs with Christ, called to be his voice. We are the recipients of his salvation, given to us through his great sacrifice. We are his beloved bride. We were poor but are now made spiritually rich. Through his Holy Spirit we have a life that will last throughout eternity. What excellent blessings he has given those called by his name!

Grace upon Grace

Proclaim Christ's excellence to someone who may be stuck in darkness.

Crucified with Christ

He died for everyone so that those who receive his new life will no longer live for themselves. Instead, they will live for Christ, who died and was raised for them.

2 CORINTHIANS 5:15 NLT

The accident victim was cloaked in confusion, but she vaguely recalled speeding. With the cold asphalt under her body, Naomi felt someone compressing her chest. The sound of sirens filled her ears as heaviness in her head and the impact of the medication lulled her to sleep. Later that day when Naomi awoke, the doctor said she should have died, but to his amazement, she was given another chance at life.

When we repent and receive Jesus as Lord and Savior, we are brought from death to life. We are indwelled by his Holy Spirit; we're a new creation yet still in the flesh. We have the choice to sin, but we desire to please the Father. We are yoked with his Son who inspires us to become less like our former selves and more like him. We have experienced a rebirth that leads to a transformation that changes us into the likeness of Jesus.

Grace upon Grace

Ask Jesus to help you live for him
and ask for grace when you fail.

One With Jesus

As many as received Him, to them He gave the right to become children of God, to those who believe in His name.

JOHN 1:12 NASB

Leah wanted her vows to be the most amazing words she had ever spoken. The writing had to be perfect. She wanted to convey everything that had made her fall in love with her groom, whom she knew so well. Sandon made her laugh and encouraged her to always see the glass half full. She trusted him; she felt loved and safe with him. When the day came, the look in Sandon's eyes told Leah that the words she spoke were sealed in his heart forever.

When we give ourselves over in total surrender to Jesus, we are sealed forevermore as his children. We bear the name, *Christ follower*, and we want his life to indwell ours. We join a large family in the body of Christ. We are his bride, and he is our bridegroom. We believe all he did and said, and trust that we will forever be with him. Through the acceptance of his salvation and our faith in his name, we are one with Jesus.

Grace upon Grace

Rejoice in the fact that Christ's work on the cross enabled you to become a child of God.

His Confidantes

> "No longer do I call you servants, for a servant does not know what his master is doing; but I have called you friends, for all things that I heard from My Father I have made known to you."

JOHN 15:15 NKJV

Temperance was summoned into the CEO's office. She went, but with trepidation. There had been watercooler talk of layoffs, and she was fearing the worst. Temperence sat across from him and tried to hide her relief as he told her he wanted to discuss some confidential re-organization plans with her. He had reviewed her work ethics and found her to be trustworthy, hard-working, and respected. He felt he could share his new strategies with her, and she could be part of the implementation.

When Jesus was speaking to his disciples, he called them his confidants. Once we become believers, we are no longer in the dark about spiritual things. It is a growing process, but nothing is hidden from us. We can ask God anything. We are called friends of Christ, brought into ministry in tandem with him.

Grace upon Grace

Read God's words to you; he calls you his friend.

Life Without End

You died to this life, and your real life
is hidden with Christ in God.

COLOSSIANS 3:3 NLT

It was odd for Patsy, one of the popular girls, to be sitting at home alone on a Friday night. In past times, she would be out all hours enjoying a loud, rowdy lifestyle. She had a gang of comrades who could party as hard as she could. Now that she knew Jesus, the friends had dispersed. They started whispering behind her back that she had become "one of those." She felt rejected and deserted by her companions. But then Patsy read in Scripture that she had died to this life. She realized it was true. She felt an intimacy and companionship with Christ that she had never experienced with the wild crowd.

When we come to know Jesus, it's a glorious moment of forgiveness, acceptance, and realization. Suddenly, we are loved more than we had ever known before. As we start to testify, some aspects of our lives change. Many acquaintances abandon us because of our faith. But we are most blessed despite the shunning, for we are new creations in Christ.

Grace upon Grace

Stand with Jesus, the author of grace, today and forever.

Live by Faith

You are all sons and daughters of God
through faith in Christ Jesus.

GALATIANS 3:26 CSB

As the youngest child and only girl, LucyAnne's brothers loved to tease her relentlessly. She was tough, though. Normally she could give back as well as they gave. One incident, however, left her defenseless. When they told her she wasn't a real member of the family but was left on their doorstep as a baby, she burst out, "That's not true! You are rotten liars!" Once the parents heard about the boys' lie, they reassured LucyAnne that she was not an abandoned baby, and her brothers suffered the consequences of their teasing.

If we are in Christ, we can be assured that we are God's children. He bought us with his blood, sealed us with his Holy Spirit, and secured us with a salvation that is irreversible. As we grow daily through prayer, studying his Word, and living a surrendered life for him, our confidence as his children grows and our light for him shines brighter!

Grace upon Grace

Let the fact that you are God's child strengthen your faith.

Family of God

You are the body of Christ
and individually members of it.

1 CORINTHIANS 12:27 ESV

Although they were not blood relatives, each one in the
Bible study group felt as though they were family. Every
Wednesday night when they met up, they would bare
their hearts. They believed they were the body of Christ,
and they proved it through their service and love for each
one present. They helped carry one another's burdens
and stepped up if anyone had a need. As they continued
to meet, share, and grow in the knowledge of Jesus, they
spread his fragrance everywhere they went.

As Christ followers, we're to be humble, putting others
ahead of ourselves. Philippians 2:5-11 tells us we are to
have the same attitude as Jesus did, not counting himself
as better than anyone, but humbling himself to the point
of death on a cross. If he did that for us, we certainly must
serve in the same manner. The church works well when
love for Jesus and selflessness is the driving force.

Humbly serve your family in Christ, as Jesus did for you.

Righteousness of God

In reference to your former way of life, you are to rid
yourselves of the old self, which is being corrupted in
accordance with the lusts of deceit, and that you are to
be renewed in the spirit of your minds, and to put on the
new self, which in the likeness of God has been created in
righteousness and holiness of the truth.

EPHESIANS 4:22-24 NASB

Old habits die hard. In Kaylee's case, she carried the weight
of her former failings like it was a five-hundred-pound
barbell. She knew that in Christ she could withstand
temptation, but the former pleasures still flaunted her with
memories. Kaylee asked God to help her don her spiritual
battle gear so she could deflect all the enemy's arrows. She
wanted to live her position as a new creation in Christ by
putting away her old life to live in the righteous perfection
of his truth.

We've been made the righteousness of God in Christ. We
have power through his Spirit to defeat Satan's schemes and
to shut out the powers of darkness. We are one with Jesus.
His ability enables us to defeat all that tempts us.

Grace upon Grace

*Reject your old, former life in favor of a new,
transformed life in Christ.*

His Great Care

He is our God and we are the people of his pasture,
the flock under his care.

PSALM 95:7 NIV

A shepherd's main job is the sheep's welfare. In biblical
times, the shepherd was on call day and night. He would
sleep near the flock to protect them. He carried a rod to
beat off any wild animals and a staff to redirect those sheep
who would tend to wander off. He was responsible for
finding the best pastures for food and water to drink. He
would groom them by sheering their fleece and removing
any disease-carrying insects. Like David, shepherds
carried a sling and some stones so they could deter lurking
predators. The shepherd's life was committed to his sheep.

The Lord is our shepherd who watches over us and who
will never forsake us. He protects us and guides us. When
we lack what we need, he gives us good gifts. If we wander
off the path, he draws us back. We can't save ourselves, so
he gave his life to redeem us. Jesus is the true shepherd.
Thankfully, we are the sheep that he adores.

Grace upon Grace

Thank Jesus specifically for his great care and love for you.

The Precious Blood

You were bought at a price; therefore glorify God in your body and in your spirit, which are God's.

1 CORINTHIANS 6:20 NKJV

As newlyweds, Rosalee and Sully had filet mignon taste on a hot dog budget. They knew if they were ever going to afford their first home on the way to their dream home they would have to live frugally. Instead of fancy restaurants, they opted for staying in and having dinner by candlelight. After being diligent for a few years, Rosalee and Sully bought their first home. They spent many hours fixing it up and taking care of it. Before long they were rewarded when it sold for the exact amount they needed for a down payment on their dream home.

As children of God, we were acquired with the precious blood of Jesus. Our bodies are his temple, filled with his Holy Spirit. It is our charge to honor God with how we care for ourselves spiritually, mentally, and physically. Every choice we make should be aligned with the instruction of the Bible to further our growth in Christ. Whatever we do in word or deed, may our number goal be to bring honor to our God.

Grace upon Grace

Remind yourself daily of the price Christ paid on the cross for you.

Proclaim Him

Be exalted, O God, above the highest heavens!
May your glory shine over all the earth.

PSALM 57:5 NLT

Our world likes to put high-profile people on a pedestal. Whether it be movie stars, politicians, music artists, or sports figures we ooh and ah at their stellar persona. We consider them to be a better breed. Some fans even fashion their own interests after their idol's examples in clothing, cosmetics, or material goods. On the occasion that a celebrity falls from grace, there are always others waiting in the wings to step into their spotlight.

God alone is good, faithful, and all-powerful. He is the only one deserving of our admiration. He created us for his pleasure, so we, his children, will worship him and not one another. Never give what is God's to man; reserve your dedication for your heavenly Father. Proclaim him as holy and righteous: the one true God whose glory will shine for eternity.

Grace upon Grace

Let your heart and mouth sing of God's goodness.

God's Image

God created man in his own image;
he created him in the image of God;
he created them male and female.

GENESIS 1:27 CSB

Typically, Juliette walked to work along the city streets ignoring all the people. But today, she had an epiphany which rocked her to her core. She had been investigating her faith, and a friend advised her to read about creation. She realized that every person who crossed her path was made in the image of the Creator. This caused her to pause and think of God when she looked into the face of her fellow man.

When we discount people, we are missing God's masterpiece. Being made in the image of God is nothing short of magnificent. The question in each person's life is, "What will the conclusion be about salvation in Jesus?" Will people decide for him or against him? Notice the people you see today and remind yourself that someday each of them will meet God and account for their decision about him. Honor the one they are made like by sharing the gospel, for he desires everyone to know him.

Grace upon Grace

When you look at people, see them as God created them, in his image.

Citizen of Heaven

Our citizenship is in heaven, from which we also eagerly
wait for the Savior, the Lord Jesus Christ.

PHILIPPIANS 3:20 NKJV

It had always been the Purdue family's dream to immigrate
to the United States. They were certain they could then
live a life of opportunity. Their goal was to become official
citizens; they constantly studied and quizzed each other on
the questions they would be tested on. The day came for the
test, and they passed with flying colors. Next, the Purdues
would attend the naturalization ceremony and take the oath
of allegiance—the final step to becoming official citizens.

The day we accept Jesus Christ as our Savior, we become a
citizen of heaven. We may have many years left on earth,
but our salvation joins us to the body of Christ. We must
be careful not to get caught up in the cares of this world or
align ourselves with it. Our residency has been transferred
to heaven. Someday soon Christ will return to take us home
to live with him in paradise.

Grace upon Grace

Imagine how glorious it will be to live with Christ in heaven!

Loving Intervention

In him we have redemption through his blood,
the forgiveness of our trespasses,
according to the riches of his grace.

EPHESIANS 1:7 ESV

Taylor and Oakley ventured to California for spring break.
They idolized Mark, a young star, and in hopes of seeing
him, they secured a Hollywood Stars' Homes Map. When
they found his address, they noticed a limo with the door
open in the driveway. Taylor and Oakley ran across Mark's
property to get an autograph, but before they could get too
close, security intercepted them. The celebrity watched the
bodyguards while he exited his limo and then interceded.
He excused the girls' intrusion and thanked them for being
fans. He then placed his arms around their shoulders so
they could snap a selfie.

If we tried to gain entrance into heaven by sneaking, we
wouldn't be allowed in. Unlike the girls who got onto the
star's property, our own efforts will never gain us a place
in God's kingdom. We can only open heaven's door by
receiving forgiveness from God. That happens when we
repent and accept the work of Christ on the cross.

Grace upon Grace

Consider the riches of Christ's grace for you.

Spiritual Benefits

Blessed be the God and Father of our Lord Jesus Christ,
who has blessed us with every spiritual blessing in the
heavenly places in Christ.

EPHESIANS 1:3 NKJV

There were all kinds of perks that came with Blake's promotion. Her new title garnered her a large expense account, opportunities to be a keynote speaker, and a hefty honorarium at the conventions she would attend. She would meet with the top executives in the country. It immediately catapulted Blake to a position of honor and prestige. She was honestly taken aback by all the favor she was given and accepted it gratefully.

When we ask Jesus into our hearts, it comes with an enormous number of undeserved heavenly blessings. We are forgiven for our sins, sealed with the Holy Spirit, and adopted into the Father's family as heirs with Christ. He has not withheld one spiritual benefit from us but has given us everything through his Son. Let's thank him continually.

Grace upon Grace

Don't ever stop thanking Jesus for choosing you.

He Chose Us

"You did not choose Me but I chose you, and appointed you that you would go and bear fruit, and that your fruit would remain, so that whatever you ask of the Father in My name He may give to you."

JOHN 15:16 NASB

It was the day for the dreaded dodgeball game. That meant the young athletes would all have to line up and wait to hear their names called by the two captains. Would they have the relief of being named quickly, or would they suffer the humiliation of standing as one of the last ones called?

Jesus said that we did not choose him; he chose us. That doesn't eliminate the fact that we willingly receive him as Savior. In view of the difficult doctrine of election, however, we must have childlike faith. To be chosen by God is beyond our understanding, yet we rejoice immensely in it. We are now invited to ask anything of God in Jesus' name and receive it. As the chosen people, we are called to do good works that endure. Belonging to Christ comes with joy as well as submission to the One who has captured our hearts.

Grace upon Grace

Work hard to bear good fruit that brings glory to Jesus' name.

Remaining in Union

You also are complete through your union with Christ,
who is the head over every ruler and authority.

COLOSSIANS 2:10 NLT

As Alaina moved the tassel from one side of her
mortarboard to the other, her time as a master's program
student was finished. She was about to become a human
resources manager at a large technical firm. She envisioned
a corner office, a staff of eager underlings, and the ability
to handle any disputes, all in a day's work. When Alaina
arrived for her first day in her shiny new position, she
learned that on-the-job dilemmas are very different from
the classroom ideal. She needed to lean on her superior for
real-world support.

In Christ, we're given everything required for salvation.
There's nothing we need to do except repent and ask for the
saving blood of the Savior. We have an internal guide in the
Holy Spirit who directs us. As King, Jesus fills us with his
power and authority to do his will. It is our responsibility
to pursue knowledge in the Word and to seek maturity in
Christ. If we seek to honor him, praying to become holy as
he is holy, he will fulfill the plans he has for us.

Grace upon Grace

*Because you are complete in Christ,
he can help you carry out his will.*

We Win

In all these things we are more than conquerors
through him who loved us.

ROMANS 8:37 CSB

The team prepared diligently for the final championship.
They looked to their beloved coach for strength, knowing
he could lead them to victory. But on the night of the big
event, Coach had an accident which landed him in the
hospital. Knowing he had given them all they needed to
compete successfully, the team ran onto the field. Even
without his presence, they knew what to do to honor the
teaching and training of their coach.

If you are a student of the Word, you know how it all
ends—in Christ, we are victors! Yet for those without
Jesus, judgment day will be the greatest defeat. If you have
not received the Savior yet, all you need to do is read the
account of his crucifixion and resurrection to know that
he defied death and offered forgiveness and eternal life. In
John 3:16, it explains that God so loved the world that he
wants to save us through the cross of Jesus. For those who
believe in him, we already know that in the end we win for
all eternity.

Grace upon Grace

*You never need to fear being overcome by sin
because you have victory in Christ!*

Steadfast Love and Mercy

He made known His ways to Moses,
His deeds to the sons of Israel.

PSALM 103:7 NASB

Finley's mama had told her every night as they prayed that God loved her and made her for a special purpose. God would always be with her, and he would never leave her side. The Father would watch over her in the night and walk with her in the day. Jesus died to save her and if she would live for him, she could look forward to an eternal relationship as his treasured child. Finley could spend a lifetime learning about his steadfast lovingkindness.

Psalm 103 speaks of how God made himself known to Israel. He revealed his grace and performed miraculous works on their behalf. He spoke of a coming Redeemer who would save them from the pit of darkness and heal them of their iniquities. He was provider, protector, and shepherd to his people. We too, are his children, and he treats us with the same mercy by his great gift of salvation. We're undeserving, yet he views each of us with the greatest love of all.

Grace upon Grace

Show God love for the grace he has revealed to you.

Eternal Reconciliation

We are therefore Christ's ambassadors, as though God were making his appeal through us. We implore you on Christ's behalf: Be reconciled to God.

2 CORINTHIANS 5:20 NIV

The mayor stood on the platform addressing the disheartened crowd. They longed for positive direction after surviving a great tragedy. He encouraged the citizens to vote in a task force to strategize for future calamities. He begged the townspeople to work alongside the authorities because they had faced dangers on their behalf; they should report trouble immediately if they suspected anything. If they acted wisely as a community, it could result in saving many lives.

As followers of Jesus, we must share the solution to spiritual death. We cannot keep the message of reconciliation that Paul spoke about just to ourselves. We are charged with speaking about the truth of Jesus' sacrifice. People need to know that the only way anyone can be saved is through the life, death, and resurrection of Jesus. We must step into our positions as diplomats for Christ and work to bring others into the kingdom.

Grace upon Grace

Appeal to a loved one who needs to receive Christ's grace personally.

Regenerated to New Life

He raised us from the dead along with Christ and seated us
with him in the heavenly realms because we are united with
Christ Jesus.

EPHESIANS 2:6 NLT

Rachelle entered the venue and quietly found a seat in
the back. She was overcome with excitement to hear her
boyfriend, Tray, speak in front of such a distinguished
group. She glanced around the room and felt out of place
among so many people who had accomplished great things
and been recognized publicly for their achievements. When
Rachelle was approached by an usher to come sit alongside
Tray on the dais, she was humbled and honored.

When we commit ourselves to Christ and receive his
forgiveness and salvation, we are regenerated into new life
in him. We then belong to him and are filled with his Spirit;
we are no longer dead in our sin. God graciously seats us
with Christ where we are citizens with him in the heavenly
kingdom.

Grace upon Grace

*Be overwhelmed with gratitude for the grace
that made you an heir with Christ.*

No Longer Slaves

We know that our old self was crucified with him so that the body of sin might be rendered powerless so that we may no longer be enslaved to sin.

ROMANS 6:6 CSB

Nala was anxious about the procedure on her back. She had rods implanted years ago now and had become accustomed to their presence. To be rid of them would be the greatest relief. She often felt imprisoned by the metal and restricted from so many activities. Now after some physical therapy, Nala would learn to move freely and enjoy doing things that had been disallowed previously. She had hope for the future and no longer felt deprived of a full life.

Those who believe in Christ have been transformed. Their bodies of sin were put to death on the cross. Evil desires have been annihilated and they never have to return to the muck and mire of their former selves. They have passed from death to life. Believers can turn their backs on lust and grow in maturity with God's moral law which leads toward purity. When old ways tempt you, remember that, through Christ, you have died to those things, and you may call on the powerful name of Jesus.

Grace upon Grace

Call on the power of Jesus to live free from sin.

Confident Access

> This was according to the eternal purpose that he has realized in Christ Jesus our Lord, in whom we have boldness and access with confidence through our faith in him.
>
> EPHESIANS 3:11-12 ESV

For many years, the truth was hidden. The Ellison family was content, and the children didn't want for anything because they were so loved. As they grew and at the proper time, they were told the secret. They were shocked to find out that they were actually very wealthy, but the children appreciated that they were raised to know Jesus and to live simply. Their parents had decided before they were born to withhold the truth so their children would trust in Christ alone and not worldly advantages.

The mystery of God's redemptive purpose for our salvation was made known in the sacrifice and resurrection of Jesus. Once the cross and its plan were completed, we can go confidently to Jesus for forgiveness and the gift of eternal life. Through faith, we become new creatures, endowed with the divine ability to live bold lives on behalf of Jesus. God provided for man's sin before the creation of the world. He was thinking of you when he made his plan.

Grace upon Grace

Think of the sacrificial love that has brought you salvation and confident access to God's throne.

Never Covet

Let us not become conceited,
provoking and envying each other.

GALATIANS 5:26 NIV

Mariana thought she'd be the first of her friends to get married. Now, Wren was beating her to the altar. Wren's fiancé was a high-profile executive who came from old money. They would start married life with a gorgeous home and all the toys. It wasn't fair! Unfortunately, Mariana started to resent her lifelong friend. She was chosen to be the maid of honor, but she skimped on the shower. She knew Wren had more than she deserved already. On the wedding day, Mariana gossiped about Wren and her groom. Her jealousy was obvious to everyone, and that devastated the bride.

How often do we feel slighted because someone has more than we have? Our jealousy consumes us, and we become miserable. Our actions come back to bite us, though, because if we are known to be vindictive, we are the ones who suffer. People do not want to be around those who gossip and malign others to elevate themselves. To honor God, we must love as he loves and refuse to be covetous.

Grace upon Grace

*Be careful not to covet the lives and possessions of others,
but to be thankful for all you have.*

First in Mind

If then you were raised with Christ, seek those things which
are above, where Christ is, sitting at the right hand of God.
Set your mind on things above, not on things on the earth.

COLOSSIANS 3:1-2 NKJV

As a new believer, Phoebe realized many things in her
life needed to take a backseat, and some things must be
outright eliminated. She had been a vibrant part of the
world before her conversion. She was a party girl who
always wore the latest fashions and hung with prestigious
people. Her presence at all the events was in high demand.
Phoebe now saw these things as insignificant compared
to a life with Christ. She chose to live for God's kingdom,
seeking to be a witness and serving others. The radical
change in her brought many of her acquaintances to Jesus.

As Christians, anything this world has to offer will pale
in comparison to heavenly things. Our allegiance and our
efforts should be solely aimed toward God's kingdom.
When we concentrate on things from above, we have peace,
hope, and joy. We are ready to speak about what's first in
our hearts and our minds—Jesus.

Grace upon Grace

*Focus on heaven and mindfully store up treasures
in God's kingdom.*

He Never Sinned

God made Christ, who never sinned,
to be the offering for our sin,
so that we could be made right with God through Christ.

2 Corinthians 5:21 nlt

Have you ever had a friend take the blame for you? If you have, you might have felt either grateful or remorseful. Consider someone is protecting us from a dire situation and they step into our place so that we need not bear the consequences. Wouldn't you feel indebted to that person? Would you want to do the same for them?

Jesus took our place and our punishment. Dictionaries define a whipping boy as one who bears the punishment for the prince. The Savior was beaten, spit upon, and nailed to a cross that should have been ours. Out of the most tremendous love, God substituted him in our stead, and he went willingly. He never sinned, yet he took on our sin so we can be forgiven. We did nothing to deserve this. What breathtaking grace! In return, if we love him, we must give up our lives for him so we can find it anew, giving every minute to bring him glory.

Grace upon Grace

Pick up your cross and follow Christ wholeheartedly.

Overwhelmed

Blessed is the God and Father of our Lord Jesus Christ, who has blessed us with every spiritual blessing in the heavens in Christ. For he chose us in him, before the foundation of the world, to be holy and blameless in love before him.

EPHESIANS 1:3-4 CSB

Lola was awestruck by the attention she received on her birthday. She received cards, gifts, and visitors wanting to celebrate with her. It blessed her enormously! She was humbled by the time they spent coming up with so many ways to make her feel loved. Lola wouldn't let this experience go to waste; she was determined to show the same devotion to everyone who had esteemed her.

When we come to Christ, we are overwhelmed by the Lord's blessings which exceed anything we could have ever desired. We weren't even the ones who made the choice initially to be put in the position to receive such grace. God, himself, chose us. We're redeemed and adopted as the Father's children. We join Jesus as beneficiaries of all heaven has to offer.

Grace upon Grace

Let thankfulness fill your heart as you are overwhelmed by all Christ has done for you.

Daily Consistent Time

Put on then, as God's chosen ones, holy and beloved, compassionate hearts, kindness, humility, meekness, and patience.

COLOSSIANS 3:12 ESV

Both Journey and Lilith were leaders in the church ladies' ministry. Most of the choices for Bible studies, fellowship events, and outreach efforts fell to their discretion. Journey led with a sincere spirit and loved Jesus wholeheartedly. Lilith seemed to be simulating her walk with Christ; she seemed disingenuous, often grating on others. Finally, the Spirit-filled Journey confronted Lilith, and she confessed that she spent more time creating activities than being with the Savior. She humbly asked for counsel. Journey and Lilith talked and prayed about how she could dedicate more time to her personal relationship with Jesus.

We're told to put on the character of Christ. This conveys decisive action on our part. We can't expect to mature in him and be like him if we don't devote daily, consistent time to prayer and the reading of the Word. We must sit at his feet and commit ourselves to learn from him.

Grace upon Grace

Never hesitate to call on Christ; you are his chosen one.

Image of Christ

The one who joins himself to the Lord
is one spirit with Him.

1 CORINTHIANS 6:17 NASB

Raegan and Dakota were so eager to be joined in matrimony and to become one as God had designed them to be. They had remained pure for marriage because they both wanted to please the Lord. To understand oneness of spirit, they studied what it meant to be one with Jesus. This aligned with their understanding of becoming united as man and wife. They spent hours learning the meaning of the special marriage union, and they were rewarded with a new closeness to Jesus and a deep love for each other.

Becoming a believer in Christ establishes an integration of his spirit with ours. We carry the life of Jesus in us; we represent who he is. Everything we do, good or bad, brings the Savior into the experience with us. We can leave a sweet or sour smell, depending on our choices. We should petition to be holy as he is holy, knowing our holiness only comes from him. Avoid sin, confess it quickly when it happens, and pray daily to be conformed ever more to the image of Christ.

Grace upon Grace

Represent Jesus well and bring others to him.

November

Prepare your hearts and minds for action! Stay alert and fix your hope firmly on the marvelous grace that is coming to you. For when Jesus Christ is unveiled, a greater measure of grace will be released to you.

1 PETER 1:13 TPT

Carry His Light

> "You are the light of the world.
> A city set on a hill cannot be hidden."
>
> MATTHEW 5:14 NASB

Heather was determined not to keep what she knew to herself. She found the answer to defying death; to resist the urge to share it with others would be criminal in her mind. She had felt like she was dying before her salvation. She had looked everywhere for a miracle and decided at one point that everything was hopeless. Then a friend approached her asking for forgiveness for not sharing the truth that had saved her. Once Heather had made the transition from death to life, she refused to hold back from anyone her knowledge of salvation.

Disciples of Christ carry his light within them. When we allow that light to radiate through our good works, it's like a lamp that guides others to the Savior. By our testimonies we illuminate the kingdom of heaven for those who have not yet found their way there.

Grace upon Grace

Shine Jesus' light to everyone who crosses your path.

A Sacred Family

You are no longer a slave but a son,
and if a son, then an heir of God through Christ.

GALATIANS 4:7 NKJV

Travis was to be released from the juvenile detention home
for foster kids. He'd been placed there after stealing a bag of
chips when he was extremely hungry. An older couple, the
Jansons, offered to take him in for a short time until other
arrangements could be made. Many months passed and
the Jansons came to care deeply for Travis. They shared the
love of Christ with him and prayed for his salvation. They
approached him, saying that since they had been adopted as
God's children through Christ, they believed God wanted
them to adopt him as their son. Travis cried tears of joy and
gratitude for his new forever family.

We are no longer slaves to sin; we have been adopted as
God's children and are joint heirs with Christ. We have a
sacred family including the patriarchs, the New Testament
disciples, and the beloved church. We have an Abba that
we can run to any time, and he will welcome us with loving
arms. As the bride of Christ, we will one day live together as
one big, blessed family!

Grace upon Grace

*Be thankful that you have been made a child of God
and given a spiritual family.*

Everything Changed

You have been united with Christ Jesus. Once you were far
away from God, but now you have been brought near to
him through the blood of Christ.

EPHESIANS 2:13 NLT

The thought of anything religious was ridiculous to Stevie.
She was always the one joking about the people she called
"self-righteous." She lived an exciting life, but secretly she
was miserable. She feared the future and being left alone.
Stevie knew one particular person, however, who was
always peaceful and joyful. When she questioned Gina, she
was told the greatest love story of all. The cynical Stevie
gave her heart to Jesus right then and came to understand
how loved and safe she was now that she belonged to him.

Most of us can remember a time when we lived for
ourselves and gave little thought to the things of God. We
maybe even believed he existed, but we didn't have much
interest beyond that. Once we heard and believed the
gospel, everything changed. We received the assurance that
we are sealed for eternity, and we experienced the peace
that passes understanding.

Grace upon Grace

*Think of how Jesus pursues you, forgives you,
and brings you near to him.*

Following Him

All who are led by the Spirit of God are sons of God.

ROMANS 8:14 ESV

Pieter prided himself as a rebel; someone who swam upstream; a person who went against the current of religious thought; a guy who found his own way. He was certain he'd be successful in life by following what he knew to be best. He had his own definition of right and wrong. But after years of floundering through life, Pieter found that those people who had been led up the religious garden path were the ones who had flourished! They weren't all rich or in perfect health, but they were all happy, or rather, content. Maybe his idea of truth was incorrect. He knew he had to investigate. He started with the people who were joyful and upright; they were the ones who had found true faith in Jesus.

When we're led by his Holy Spirit, the evidence of who we belong to can be seen by everyone. We're not orphans; we're his children. We're not slaves; we're his offspring. We lack nothing for he has given us everything in Christ.

Grace upon Grace

Allow yourself to be led by the Holy Spirit.

Cry Out to Abba

You did not receive a spirit of slavery to fall back into fear.
Instead, you received the Spirit of adoption, by whom we
cry out, "Abba, Father!" The Spirit himself testifies together
with our spirit that we are God's children.

ROMANS 8:15-16 CSB

It was the first night that the little twins were with their
new forever family. They felt relieved to be adopted yet still
distanced. As the parents tucked them in bed, they prayed,
asking God to watch over them. The children hoped that
they could accept they were finally where they belonged.
When a nightmare woke one of them up, they both started
to cry. Mom and Dad rushed in, held them in their arms
and assured them they would always be there to protect
them. That's when they started to believe they were home.

Living in this world as believers we still have times when we
feel far from God. We can get wrapped up in the worries of
the world, allowing fear to set in. If we will cry out to our
Abba, he reminds us compassionately that he never left. As
we cozy up to our Father, his Spirit reassures us that he has
won the battle, made us his own, and we are sealed safely in
his arms.

Grace upon Grace

Remember that God has adopted you, and he is a good Father.

Spiritual Battle

Praise be to the LORD my Rock
who trains my hands for war,
my fingers for battle.

PSALM 144:1 NIV

Daphne had always fought a war with her weight. Losing
anything was a constant battle. She convinced a friend,
Adaline, to join her at a women's bootcamp that guaranteed
to get them in shape, and Daphne hoped she would finally
overcome her weight war. The exercise was tough, but in
the end, she learned about self-control, preparing healthy
meals, and how being active was a true asset. The training
paid off and she found success over this lifelong struggle.

Our preparation to do spiritual battle is found in Scripture.
Add the power of God to your fervent prayer, and you will
be ready to shut down the devil's diabolical deeds.

*Put on your armor so you are prepared
to destroy Satan's evil plans for you.*

Shut Satan Down

We do not wrestle against flesh and blood, but against principalities, against powers, against the rulers of the darkness of this age, against spiritual hosts of wickedness in the heavenly places.

EPHESIANS 6:12 NKJV

Eustace and Kali's first of many struggles were minor inconveniences like failing appliances. Next, they caught the virus that was going around. The lies and the gossip about them, though, was the thing that bothered them most. Eustace and Kali believed these people were their friends! They started to get depressed and angry. Then they remembered what the pastor had said about Satan using people to offend us in a demonic attack. They decided to pray for those who hurt them and place their trust in God to deliver them from their struggles. They then committed Ephesians 6:12 to memory.

We are not at war with people. We're in a spiritual battle with the enemy of our souls and his army of demons. We must recognize this and clothe ourselves with God's armor to deflect all the devil's tactics. Ask for wisdom to identify your real adversary, and it's usually not the people around you.

Grace upon Grace

Do not hold grudges; fight directly with the source of your pain.

The Church

We no longer see each other in our former state—Jew or non-Jew, rich or poor, male or female—because we're all one through our union with Jesus Christ.

GALATIANS 3:28 TPT

The multi-cultural group tended to stay within their own smaller groups. It was comfortable, and not risky. They didn't realize they were missing out on the larger group's fellowship if they would only intermingle with each other. They didn't get to engage in each other's traditions or find out how much they truly had in common. When one member decided to mix it up, others joined in. As they opened their hearts and minds to their differences, they began to understand their similarities as well. Soon they were a big, beautiful, diverse community.

As the church, the body of Christ, we are created to be a family that is joined together by his saving grace. Whether we are a man or a woman, one ethnicity or another, and of whatever social status, we are first and foremost children of God. If we accept and love one another, we understand that we are all joined as one with Christ.

Grace upon Grace

Love and support members of the body of Christ.

Specifically Chosen

We know, brothers loved by God,
that he has chosen you.

1 THESSALONIANS 1:4 ESV

The coordinator of the retreat had searched long and hard, hoping to find the perfect presenter for the weekend. He finally found a riveting speaker, and the crowd enthusiastically took notes on everything she said. The coordinator was so glad he had booked this woman because the audience was obviously enthralled. Scripture was shared in a way that made it come alive, and the takeaways were applicable and life changing. Everyone knew that this woman was chosen for such a time and event as this.

There is no greater joy than to be chosen as a child of God. It carries with it great responsibility and humility. The Creator, the Lord most high, personally and specifically desires us. If we could comprehend that truth in all its wonder, would we live differently? We need to pray that we will understand our election fully and live to serve the almighty God who selected us for such a time as this.

Grace upon Grace

Be reassured that God's love for you is steadfast.

Blood of Christ

You were bought with a price;
do not become slaves of human beings.

1 CORINTHIANS 7:23 NIV

Paige tried to hide her sin from her family. She had various places where she would conceal the bottles. She had become an expert at disguising the fact that she was under the influence. They knew something was different—she was a bit more overt. But the family didn't want to offend her, so they held their tongues. Eventually, Paige's brother could no longer sit by without some kind of a confrontation. She belonged to this family, and besides, he wanted her to be safe. Paige was compromising her health and her reputation.

The blood of Christ was the costliest compensation. Nothing else but the blood that flowed from his torn skin would be sufficient payment for our sin. Our lives have been purchased and everything we say and do reflects upon our Savior. We want to bring him glory with every breath and shower him with our gratitude for all he's given us. Thank you, Jesus, for your precious body, sacrificed to pay the price that brought us peace.

Grace upon Grace

Let Christ's sacrifice shape the way you live for him.

Shout His Goodness

You are a people holy to the LORD your God. The LORD
your God has chosen you out of all the peoples on the face
of the earth to be his people, his treasured possession.

DEUTERONOMY 7:6 NIV

Four-year-old Talia was brought to the safe house in
the middle of the night by the authorities. She was in a
domestic situation that demanded she be separated from
her parents, and they sadly waived their rights. In her
temporary home afterward, Talia would ask whenever a
woman visited if she was her new mommy. One day her
question was answered with a yes! A loving lady walked
in and arranged to take little Talia home to her family. She
scooped her up in her arms and told the child she had
chosen her to be her daughter.

When Abba adopted us, he chose us before the formation
of the world. He established that we would be his precious
possession, his elect. We were sealed through salvation in
Christ, saved from damnation and cloaked in his mercy.
He graciously handed us his holiness and placed a robe of
righteousness over our souls. What joy to sing his praises
and to shout his goodness from the rooftops.

Grace upon Grace

*Boast about the God who chose you
before you could choose him.*

His Divine Power

In Him dwells all the fullness of the Godhead bodily;
and you are complete in Him, who is the head of all
principality and power.

COLOSSIANS 2: 9-10 NKJV

Rebecca sat in the secular college classroom and an urgency
to speak out rose in her spirit. She feared the rebuke of the
professor, so she uttered a prayer for boldness. The world
religions teacher proclaimed that Jesus was not God, but
only a good teacher. Rebecca couldn't hold back. She stood
and shared Scripture proclaiming that Jesus was God in
human flesh, had died for all humanity. He was resurrected,
and reigns in heaven as King. She implored the students
to read the living Word and learn about the Savior who
sacrificed his life to save them.

We must be ready with an answer to proclaim who Jesus
is. His undying love for the world drove him to death
on the cross. His is the only name by which any can be
redeemed, and we who know him must tell the good news.
Never doubt the influence you have in Christ. Live in faith,
demonstrating his divine power through the Spirit.

Grace upon Grace

Study God's Word to defend his truth to the world.

Eternal Reasons

One day Jesus called together his twelve disciples and gave them power and authority to cast out all demons and to heal all diseases.

LUKE 9:1 NLT

The church group laid hands on their suffering sister in Christ. They prayed and believed God for his healing power. When the miracle came, they rejoiced immensely that their dear one's health was restored. When another member became sick, they entered into battle again with prayer. God's healing this time was to take this brother home to heaven. Trusting the Lord in their sadness and through their tears they rejoiced again. They knew the Lord is good and his ways are always righteous.

We have the supernatural power to pray and do all things through Christ. He gives us the gift of faith to know nothing is impossible. When we receive a yes to our request we should fall on our faces in gratitude. We serve a God that does what is best. He works on our behalf with an eternal plan, and one day we will fully understand.

Grace upon Grace

Know that temporary pain on earth has eternal reasons.

Use His Power

"All authority has been given to me
in heaven and on earth."

MATTHEW 28:18 CSB

The employees waited anxiously to be addressed by the new boss. They heard rumors that he was demanding, detailed, and driven. Everyone wondered if he would help the company progress or bring it to ruin. When he entered the room, he moved with authority. He spoke eloquently and they hung on his every word. Acknowledging his leadership, they longed to please him. As time progressed the worked hard to follow his navigation of the company's future.

Jesus taught with such authority that no one could refute a single word he said. There was no one who could deny his miraculous power as he healed the sick and brought the dead back to life. Pompous religious leaders denied him, proving themselves to be foolish. Tax collectors, prostitutes, and the sick were the ones who recognized him as Messiah. They believed he was Israel's Redeemer, and they dedicated their lives to following him. Does he have authority in your life?

Grace upon Grace

Do a heart check to be sure Jesus has all authority in your life.

I Surrender

Submit yourselves therefore to God.
Resist the devil, and he will flee from you.

JAMES 4:7 ESV

As an eighteen-year-old girl living in her first apartment, Logan felt both excitement and trepidation. She appreciated being raised in a good Christian home, but she was also eager for her freedom. The first power outage late at night brought panic, but Logan found the flashlight and survived. The first time her boyfriend visited brought feelings she had not anticipated, but she found the courage to tell him to leave. She prayed for strength, yielding herself to God, and achieving victory over the enemy's temptations.

There are valid reasons God tells us to submit to him. Submission involves giving over control, and as Christians, we must trust our heavenly Father. We have all we need in Jesus to overcome those temptations. Scripture tells us to don the armor of God and stand firm in our faith to resist the devil. Satan's schemes are no joke. The safest way is to surrender to the Lord and determine to refuse the evil one's enticement at every turn.

Grace upon Grace

Surrender control of your life to God,
and he will protect you from the evil one.

Almighty God

You are from God, little children, and have overcome them;
because greater is He who is in you than he
who is in the world.

1 JOHN 4:4 NASB

Silas hid behind his father believing he'd be safe. This was
the first time he had seen a clown and the appearance
frightened him. When the circus performer reached around
to try to shake his hand, Silas squealed with fear. His daddy
gathered him up in his arms, assuring him that he would
shield him from any harm. The boy relaxed, believing his
dad was the strongest and greatest man alive.

God is our great protector who will never leave us or
forsake us. His steadfast love hides us in the shadow of his
wings. His plans for us are always victorious. When Satan
tries to deceive us into believing he is superior, we should
roar with laughter! He is powerless compared to Jesus. It's
impossible for the devil to do anything that could ever
thwart God's plans. Our enemy's time is limited. Someday
our heavenly Father will cast him to the pit. But our Lord
will eternally be on the throne!

Grace upon Grace

Have confidence in God as your great defender in this world.

Our Shepherd

"My sheep listen to my voice;
I know them, and they follow me."

JOHN 10:27 NIV

An accident had impaired Celeste's eyesight and getting used to walking was presenting some difficulties. She saw dimly, and she longed for someone who could guide her safely. Her physician told her about specialized training that equipped guide dogs to not only lead but also to emit a specific whine if their subject ventured toward danger. All Celeste would have to do was listen and follow the animal's voice.

Jesus is our shepherd. We are his sheep, and he loves us. He desires to guide us with his staff, so we stay on his path. He protects us from dangers with his rod, but he will also use it to discipline us for our good. He provides for our needs with his good gifts. Staying close to him leads us in his everlasting way.

Grace upon Grace

*Spend time with Jesus so you know him
and become obedient to his voice.*

Spiritual DNA

Whatever is born of God overcomes the world. And this is
the victory that has overcome the world—our faith. Who is
he who overcomes the world, but he who believes that
Jesus is the Son of God?

1 JOHN 5:4-5 NKJV

It was Gina's first marathon. Her mother had been a
champion runner, so she had hoped the talent was
inherited. She practiced hard, running many miles a day
to build her endurance. Gina had her eye on the prize and
really believed she would succeed. When the day of the
event arrived, she set her mind on the finish line and the
triumph ahead.

We have our heavenly Father's spiritual DNA in us. We
were made in his very image. Through Jesus we have
no fear of the future, for we know the victory that exists
now and the security of eternity later. Those who do not
know Jesus are wandering through this world, hopelessly
wondering why they are here. The gospel will help open
the eyes of those searching to understand why they were
created. It is the height of love to show someone the way to
forgiveness, salvation, and eternal life.

Grace upon Grace

*Have faith that you are a victorious overcomer
because of the life of Jesus within you.*

Old Temptations

When people keep on sinning, it shows that they belong to
the devil, who has been sinning since the beginning. But
the Son of God came to destroy the works of the devil.

1 John 3:8 nlt

Mackenzie had vacillated about going to church but figured
it couldn't hurt. She was suspicious when she heard the
gospel message but then thought about it as fire insurance.
Mackenzie prayed the prayer of salvation silently in her
seat, telling no one about her decision. After a brief spiritual
high, her life returned to the old ways. No pursuit of
spiritual things was anywhere on her daily list, and the old
temptations continued to win out.

Some unbelievers choose sin because of its pleasures, joking
about joining their buddies in hell where the party will rage
on. Some believers are lax about their misdeeds, thinking
they'll just pray for forgiveness later. Hebrews 10:26 says if
we keep deliberately sinning, there no longer is a sacrifice
for our sins. Loving Jesus brings a desire to reject our
transgressions and to live for him.

Grace upon Grace

*Consistently reject the deceit of the enemy; your life
is eternally united with Christ because of grace.*

Victor Overall

"The LORD will cause the enemies who rise up against you to be defeated before you. They will march out against you from one direction but flee from you in seven directions."

DEUTERONOMY 28:7 CSB

The boss asked Lauren to stay late to finish an important project. She knew it would be sketchy to walk through the parking garage alone at that time of night. She heard footsteps and moved quickly as she prayed to Jesus for protection. Lauren turned, seeing two men behind her with obvious intent in their eyes. She faced them, and the men froze. A look of fear came over them and they ran in the opposite direction. Their reaction was an answer to her prayer.

Today's verse should empower all those in Christ to have courage in their hearts. We shouldn't play fast and loose with risk, but if we find ourselves in a situation we can't avoid, have faith that Jesus is your protector. The outcome is in his hands, and he's always working on our behalf for our good. Romans 8 says nothing can separate us from God. Trust in the Lord, knowing that whatever comes your way, you're safe in the shadow of the Almighty.

Grace upon Grace

Rest in the knowledge that the Lord is your Savior, protector, and victor.

Collective Effort

Pay careful attention to yourselves and to all the flock, in which the Holy Spirit has made you overseers, to care for the church of God, which he obtained with his blood.

ACTS 20:28 ESV

Labor was harsh for Alyssa and her baby. A stuck shoulder made delivery difficult and frightening. The doctor meticulously worked to direct the child into a better position as the infant's daddy prayed. After two hours of intense concentration by all involved, movement was made, and a beautiful little boy emerged. Through blood, sweat, and tears, a new life entered a world of love because all worked together for the good of the child.

Through the blood of his broken body and resurrection, Jesus lovingly made the church his collective bride. As his treasured possession, we are to love one another with significant consideration. The care we give should be sacrificial. Our motto should be to eagerly serve, listen intently, and pray passionately.

Grace upon Grace

Be willing to step in and serve when asked to be the hands and feet of Jesus.

Assured Victory

Take up the full armor of God so that you will be able to resist on the evil day and, having done everything, to stand firm.

EPHESIANS 6:13 NASB

The weather bureau sounded the alarm that catastrophic weather was coming their way. Claire's family lived where tornados loved to wreak havoc. They knew the drill and gathered supplies for several days. They prayed for protection as they headed down to their basement and bolted the door. They could hear the howling wind and cracking trees through the concrete walls as they imagined the destruction. They interceded for neighbors and friends. They thanked God for a secure dwelling where they would be safe and sound until the storm passed.

Satan's destructive storms of attack can be defeated with God's battle plan. Wearing the armor of God with the power of the Holy Spirit and saving blood of Christ assures our victory. Going to war without this attire is foolish. Don the footwear of peace, belt of truth, and breastplate of righteousness. Carry the shield of faith and the sword of the spirit as you wear the helmet of salvation.

Grace upon Grace

Wear the armor of God and run the race for God's glory.

Power to Overcome

Do not be overcome by evil,
but overcome evil with good.

ROMANS 12:21 NIV

Nicole couldn't wait to read the popular thriller. It was a New York Times bestseller, soon to be a movie, and on the cover of many magazines. She left the bookstore with her new novel and headed home. Nicole relaxed in her favorite chair and opened the first chapter. Her senses were horrified when she read the vividly explicit torture scenes in the opening pages. The language was offensive; the perversity of the plot was shocking. Throwing the book down, she felt like she needed a shower and possibly a fast.

There are things God never intended us to see or read, but when sin entered the world, humanity became enticed by evil. Christ already won the victory. When evil invades your life, cry out to Jesus. God works everything for good and he'll give you the power to overcome.

Grace upon Grace

*Be alert not to engage in anything evil;
remain focused on Christ.*

Leave His Legacy

Whatever you do in word or deed, do all in the name of the
Lord Jesus, giving thanks to God the Father through Him.

COLOSSIANS 3:17 NKJV

Willa wanted to find a way for her life to account for
something. She loved her job and prayed to have an impact
there. On her coffee break, a co-worker, Makayla entered the
room and asked if she could join Willa. Makayla shared that
she had been watching Willa and wanted to know how she
stayed so joyful. The reason for her joy, Willa shared, and
her desire to do all things well was due to her love for Jesus.

When we're known as a Christ follower, others watch us.
They notice when our walk doesn't align with our talk. If
our heart's desire is to introduce people to Jesus, then we
should be aware of our speech and our actions. We should
check our motives before we speak or when we behave in
certain ways because those reveal our hidden intentions.
Determine to live and love like Jesus.

Grace upon Grace

Commit all you do to the Lord and leave his legacy in this life.

Humbling Ourselves

Dress yourselves in humility as you relate to one another,
for "God opposes the proud but gives grace to the humble."

1 PETER 5:5 NLT

Ainsley had come to a standstill with her mother. She felt
her mom was out of touch with reality, really behind the
times. Why wouldn't she let Ainsley camp out overnight
with her friends so they could buy tickets for a concert? Her
mom seemed excessively protective. Ainsley's mother then
explained that her decision was final and that accepting that
mandate with humility would show the needed maturity to
give her daughter more freedom in the future.

God's wisdom in placing those in the church who are
older in positions of authority is for the good of the body.
Younger generations are wise to absorb knowledge from
the people who have walked with the Lord for many years,
growing in likeness to Jesus. Hearing of their hunger and
commitment to God is inspiring. When wisdom is shared,
victories and failures provide invaluable guidance. If we
humble ourselves to learn from those who have gone before
us, we will reap great benefits.

Grace upon Grace

Live in such a way that your life benefits others.

The Rock

"I also say to you that you are Peter,
and on this rock I will build my church,
and the gates of Hades will not overpower it."

MATTHEW 16:18 CSB

Many people working behind the scenes thought that the more-vocal assistant was the one calling the shots. He was charged with keeping his finger on the pulse of what the group thought of their employer, encouraging them to support him. The boss trusted his associate to defend his reputation and to build a foundation that furthered his vision.

In Matthew 16, Jesus asked Simon Peter about what people were saying about him, and Peter defended him as the Christ. Peter went on to deliver the gospel on the day of Pentecost and the church began to thrive. The rock is Jesus. He is mentioned as the gift of salvation and the cornerstone that the church is built upon. Peter boldly represented Christ and the gospel.

Grace upon Grace

*Declare that Jesus is your Savior, the Son of God,
and the Messiah.*

Acting Blamelessly

The LORD, God is a sun and shield;
the LORD bestows favor and honor.
No good thing does he withhold
from those who walk uprightly.

PSALM 84:11 ESV

The two finalists in the competition had twenty-four hours to finish their preparations. Rosemary and Dayna entered their projects into the workshop for the next day's contest. Everything would be under the judge's noses at that point. Winning meant a large sum of money which would allow them to invest in their businesses. Rosemary was honest, but Dayna had a deceitful plot. She entered the work area after dark and altered Rosemary's presentation. The next day Dayna was barred from the challenge. The judges had checked the footage on the hidden camera to make sure nothing was disturbed overnight, and her deeds were discovered. Rosemary was awarded the prize.

Acting blamelessly means doing what is right, honoring your word even if it is inconvenient, and not slandering another person. If we want to bring glory to God, we are to live a holy existence that will demonstrate his goodness and love.

Grace upon Grace

*When you need it, ask God for help to live
a holy and righteous life.*

Complete in Christ

All Scripture is inspired by God and beneficial for teaching, rebuke, correction, for training in righteousness; so that the man or woman of God may be competent, equipped for every good work.

2 TIMOTHY 3:16-17 NASB

The character traits listed on the whiteboard were supported by accompanying verses. Every day during breakfast, the mom would read one Scripture verse and teach her children how it applied to their development and behavior. When they were grown, she looked back at those special times. She remembered the dedicated prayers which had contributed to who her children were today. She loved her work in raising godly, successful young adults. She praised God for encouraging her to stay consistent in training them by the truth of his Word.

Every answer to every problem is in the Bible. The mystery of the purpose of life is discussed in its living words and pages. We find freedom from sin, the path to obedience, and reform from sinful ways. In order to be holy as he is holy, we must conform to his righteousness.

Grace upon Grace

Crave God's written truth and ingest it until it becomes part of you.

Go to Jesus

Finally, be strong in the Lord and in his mighty power.

EPHESIANS 6:10 NIV

Fatima didn't think she could endure another moment as a patient in this place. When she decided to go ahead with the surgery, she had trusted her physician about the length of the recovery period. Of course, she had to sign a waiver accepting that sometimes things don't go as planned, but Fatima didn't think it would happen to her. Then a month turned into six months of painful rehabilitation, and she cried out to God. Remembering his Word says that his grace is sufficient, Fatima prayed for strength and submitted her health to him. She knew that the timeframe of her whole life belongs to the ultimate healer.

When we're down to our last bit of strength, it is past time to go to Jesus. If we want to remain strong in stressful situations, we must draw on his ability to get us through. Our God is more than able; he is the waymaker and miracle worker who has promised to answer when we call. He will deliver us, and he will heal us in his perfect will.

Grace upon Grace

Be strengthened by the only one who can strengthen you—
Jesus.

For Love

Peter and the other apostles answered and said:
"We ought to obey God rather than men."

ACTS 5:29 NKJV

Morris, the accountant, assured the salon owner, Kira, that everybody did things his way. Morris told her that no one ever checked these types of documents well enough to find a little fib, and it would save her a handful of cash. "The government will never catch it," he told Kira. Even though Kira was a new believer, this just didn't sit well. She'd learned enough to know that lying was a sin. Morris persisted; Kira refused. The caveat was that she got to tell him why she wouldn't cut corners—it's all because of Jesus.

When someone says a small sin won't matter, the statement is similar to the one spoken by the snake in the garden. He deceived Eve by saying, "Did God really say…?" The Bible is God's living, accurate, spoken Word. There's no argument, fact, or theory that will ever disprove it. Choosing to go along with someone's reasonings just to please them leaves you standing in the world. Always stand for Christ, obey his Word, and choose him over man.

Grace upon Grace

Resist the desire to win man's approval over God's.

December

The Lord your God is gracious and compassionate. He will not turn his face from you if you return to him.

2 CHRONICLES 30:9 NIV

Encourage One Another

You, dear friends, must build each other up in your
most holy faith, pray in the power of the Holy Spirit,
and await the mercy of our Lord Jesus Christ,
who will bring you eternal life. In this way,
you will keep yourselves safe in God's love.

JUDE 1:20-21 NLT

Reading the news became an anxious activity for Lou.
Wars, food shortage, and rising prices made life seem
entirely unpredictable. Begging God for his peace, she felt
led in her spirit to spend her time blessing other believers,
praying for the salvation of unbelievers, and looking
forward to Christ's return. As Lou did this, the concerns of
the world melted away.

Listening to the news appears to report the birth pangs of
the end times. This is not a moment for trepidation; it's an
exciting time to be alive! As the church, we're not called to
hunker down in fear, but rather to encourage one another
in the faith. His Holy Spirit gives us power for all things. He
will return to take us home in his timing, but for now, let's
stay busy encouraging each other.

Grace upon Grace

*Don't be concerned with fearful world events;
see each day as an opportunity from the Lord.*

The One

How priceless your faithful love is, God!
People take refuge in the shadow of your wings.

PSALM 36:7 CSB

A sixtieth wedding anniversary is a rare celebration. The beauty of the love shared by Stuart and Ivy which had lasted those decades was to be marveled. Their lives weren't void of hardships, and in fact, many wondered how they had survived the many trials. Their success resulted from a relationship built upon the continual love and protection of God. Faithfully committed to him and to one another, Stuart and Ivy spent a lifetime rejoicing in the presence of his peace and provision.

Our heavenly Father is constant. God's love will never change, he'll never abandon us, and he'll always call us his treasured possession. Jesus is our defender and conquering hero who loves each of us with the most overwhelming affection. When trouble comes, there are no shoulders like his. When you need a safe harbor, go to the only one who can calm the raging seas, for he will put your heart at rest.

Grace upon Grace

Thank the Lord that he is your shepherd and deliverer.

Your Champion

Help me, O Lᴏʀᴅ my God!
Save me according to your steadfast love!

PSALM 109:26 ESV

Even though Amy was surrounded by people who loved her, she felt alone. The unexpected tragedy left her feeling lost. Without any personal fortitude to right herself, Amy felt like she was living in a dark hole. Even her well-meaning friends and family weren't enough to bring her back. She was avoiding God. He would call her to trust, and she wasn't ready. After all, couldn't he have stopped this catastrophe? In the quiet of the night, Amy finally wept, asking for help, and God met her with his enduring lovingkindness.

There are times of trial when we hesitate to go to God. Maybe we're ashamed, thinking we caused the problem; maybe we're angry, thinking he could have stopped it. The truth is, he alone is our only hope. He's always working for our good even though we don't understand it at present. Always remember his great love for you which surpasses any other. He desires to be your helper, your champion, and your deliver.

Grace upon Grace

Be amazed by God's saving grace and steadfast love that loved you first.

The Lord's Favor

Do not be wise in your own eyes;
Fear the LORD and turn away from evil.

PROVERBS 3:7 NASB

Believing she could outsmart the other people in the competition, Brianne decided to purchase an item online that she was supposed to actually create. She found an obscure website so no one would discover it, and she ordered. She relaxed and waited for the delivery, fully expecting to be rewarded with the top prize. Imagine her surprise when a fellow competitor recognized the craftsmanship and called it out. The website was owned by his cousin, and that item was made by him! Brianne, the foolish one, skulked away, and once more the truth prevailed. Cheaters never win!

We come up with crazy schemes when our prideful sin nature takes over. We think we're so smart, yet we are ridiculously daft. We will only triumph when we follow God's moral laws and his commands. Truth has a way of surfacing. If we want the Lord's favor, we must pray for pure hearts, righteous motives, and true knowledge. That only comes from studying Scripture.

Grace upon Grace

Be alert for when you start to go your own sinful way.

Singing Over You

Anxiety weighs down the heart,
but a kind word cheers it up.

PROVERBS 12:25 NIV

Paisley's nails were nearly bit to the quick and sweat beaded her forehead. She was waiting for the doctor's test results, but all she could think about was how she could have done things differently. If she'd avoided certain food choices or been more attentive to the signs, maybe she would have caught this quicker. The doctor approached, telling Paisley that her tests were normal! She nearly jumped for joy! She promised to live a healthier lifestyle and he applauded her wise decision.

When life brings us unwelcome possibilities our stress levels soar. We fret and blame ourselves, and then we promise God that if he will only answer our prayers, then we will do better. He whispers, "Trust and do not fear." In his kindness, he assures us that he alone is calling the shots and we are safe in his hands. Worry overshadows faith. Believe his tender words of truth written on the pages of his Book and reaffirm in your mind and heart that he is singing over you.

Grace upon Grace

Let the Holy Spirit encourage you to replace fear with peace.

Sin Brings Death

What shall we say then?
Shall we continue in sin that grace may abound?

ROMANS 6:1 NKJV

Siobhan was a little hesitant to borrow the car without asking, but what was that saying? Oh yes—better to ask forgiveness than permission. She had been dying to drive it since her brother bought it. It was his pride and joy, and per his instructions, under no circumstances was she to get behind the wheel. Well, Siobhan would prove she could be trusted. That was until she was standing next to a police officer after rear-ending a parked car. When her brother arrived on the scene, she saw the anger on his face and realized how foolish she had been.

We have been given the greatest grace, the most extravagant mercy. If we think it is okay to willfully sin, repeatedly going through that revolving door of temptation, we are sorely mistaken. God will always and without limit forgive a repentant heart, but one that knowingly keeps choosing disobedience is using forgiveness as an easy out. God blesses those who renounce a sinful lifestyle. Sin brings death, but a faithful life for Christ brings life everlasting.

Grace upon Grace

*Make it your utmost priority to please God
and not fall for the temporary pleasures of sin.*

Put Action Behind It

Don't just listen to God's word. You must do what it says.
Otherwise, you are only fooling yourselves.

JAMES 1:22 NLT

The group of do-gooders created a list of random acts of kindness in order to challenge one another. They wanted to serve people in need. They all decided to make themselves accountable to each other; this could become a lifestyle and not a just one-time thing. Every month they met, shared a meal, and told of their opportunities that month. Bernard's head hung, though, as he shared that he'd wanted to serve and meant to follow through, but he had not made it a priority. Time escaped him and admittedly, he'd put his own desires first.

Whether it is a question of helping others or following God's commands, if we don't put our intentions into actions, they are meaningless. It is akin to letting Scripture go in one ear and out the other. We aspire to live for Jesus and to fulfill his pre-ordained plan for our lives, but we find excuses. Ask the Holy Spirit for his passion and power. Believe that God will equip you with all you need to accomplish what he has purposed for you to complete.

Grace upon Grace

Put deeds behind your words.

God Will Provide

Faith is the reality of what is hoped for,
the proof of what is not seen.

HEBREWS 11:1 CSB

Tyler and Alyssa were faithful servants of the Lord. They
had started a non-profit to minister to the poor, ending up
on the edge of poverty themselves. When they didn't have
many dollars left to stretch, they read the story in 2 Kings 4,
where the woman and her sons had only one jar of oil. She
begged Elisha to help her. He told her to borrow as many
empty containers from her neighbors as she could. She
might have thought this pointless, for vacant vessels would
not solve her problem. Yet, she took what faith she had
and gathered the jugs. Elisha told her to start pouring the
oil from her one jar into the others until they were filled.
Believing, she did it, and all the jars were filled to the brim.

The couple chose to act in faith as the woman had. They
prayed, and soon, their non-profit had donors knocking
down their doors. God provided more than they needed.
Have faith that God will provide what you need out of his
plentiful storehouse.

Grace upon Grace

*Believe with certainty that God will provide
exactly what you need.*

Careless Words

The tongue is a small part of the body,
yet it carries great power!
Just think of how a small flame
can set a huge forest ablaze.

JAMES 3:5 TPT

The Balfour couple had been planning their pioneer camping trip for weeks and could hardly wait to get on the road. The first timers easily set up their tent and unloaded the car of everything except the food. After their camp was organized, they took a long hike and enjoyed the scenery. When they returned it was dusk and they got a fire going. Since the fire was just a small flame, the outdoor newbies left it momentarily to get their food. When they returned, that little flame had become a roaring inferno that had set their camp ablaze.

Once started, fires can become uncontrollable and have devastating effects. In the same way, carelessly spoken words, harsh comments, or gossip can send shockwaves through the heart. There is great power in the tongue, and thus we must keep watchful control over everything we say. Speak love and grace and that which edifies others.

Grace upon Grace

*Speak words that will receive approval
and be pleasing to the Lord.*

Be the Example

One who is righteous is a guide to his neighbor,
but the way of the wicked leads them astray.

PROVERBS 12:26 ESV

The Thompson family was overwhelmed with their cross-country move. Their new community had been welcoming. The organizer of all the goodies was a kind woman who offered to help in any way possible. It seemed like she would make a great friend. Her teenaged son, however, had a skulking demeanor and swore often. The new family decided they would not allow their children around the boy unless they were also present.

The Bible has all the guidance needed for a good life. We should follow it ever so closely to avoid any chance of being deceived or led down the wrong path. Scripture tells us to be holy and live righteously. Our closest confidantes should be believers seeking the same attributes. When you sense that you may be the victim of someone subtly trying to entice you into sin, cease the companionship. Strive to be the example that leads others to godliness.

Grace upon Grace

*Ask the Holy Spirit to help you recognize an evildoer
and run the other way.*

Give Praise

If anyone thinks himself to be religious yet
does not bridle his tongue but deceives his own heart,
this person's religion is worthless.

JAMES 1:26 NASB

On testimonial night, the First Street Church congregation would humbly report about the good things that God had empowered them to do that month. Megan self-identified as the one who accomplished much for God's kingdom and never acknowledged the Lord as she rattled off her righteous accomplishments. The pastor called her in to discuss her presentations, tactfully suggesting that she give glory to God. That offended her, and she took her boastful spirit to another church.

If we find ourselves bragging, we must remember the one who gave us the ability to speak. We wouldn't have the breath it takes to utter a word if God didn't fill our lungs. When profit comes, humbly give praise to God for his power at work within you. Pride is subtle and it causes us to ponder how much of our own efforts brought a triumph. To stay on the side of victory, we must never take the credit but give it to the one who deserves it—our almighty God.

Grace upon Grace

Know that success is only realized through your almighty God.

Greatest Love Story

God showed his love among us: He sent his one and only Son into the world that we might live through him. This is love: not that we loved God, but that he loved us and sent his Son as an atoning sacrifice for our sins.

1 JOHN 4:9-10 NIV

Everyone adores a great love story, the author thought. She considered the romance novels she had read over the years and the details that had touched her the most. As she sat down at her computer to start the writing process, her mind kept returning to one story. There never was a more lavish love than the one exhibited at Calvary. That was a love which was unreturned by most of mankind yet poured out in such surrender it could never be surpassed.

It is almost incomprehensible to consider Christ's extraordinary love. How many of us would willingly give our child to die for a sinful person, let alone for the sins of the whole world? God demonstrated his commitment to his creation by loving us first even in our sinful state. Jesus made it possible for us to be adopted into God's family by pouring out his precious blood. This is the greatest love story ever told.

Grace upon Grace

Allow yourself to emotionally consider the Savior's love for you.

Abiding in Jesus

"Everyone assembled here will know that the LORD rescues his people, but not with sword and spear. This is the LORD's battle, and he will give you to us!"

1 SAMUEL 17:47 NLT

Jonathan realized how unprepared he was when he arrived with the ministry in the hostile third-world country. He had enlisted with a few others from his church in the US. Every nerve in his body trembled with the loud reminders from the ministry's leader to walk strictly on the road to avoid land mines. Fear started to overtake him, and he felt faint. Crying out to Jesus to quiet the voice of his enemy, he felt the power of the Holy Spirit from within. He began to praise God for the opportunity of this trip, and he was filled with peace and strength to continue. The fear left him and with it, the devil was defeated.

Scripture gives us strategies for attacks from Satan. We have victory by abiding in Jesus and refusing to yield to the enemy's lies. When we praise Jesus, the evil one will turn his tail and run; he can't handle hearing our worship. Quoting the Word out loud will also make him retreat. Through Christ, we overcome!

Grace upon Grace

Praise Jesus for the power he has given you to resist Satan.

Lead by the Spirit

Do everything without complaining and arguing so that no one can criticize you. Live clean, innocent lives as children of God, shining like bright lights in a world full of crooked and perverse people.

PHILIPPIANS 2:14-15 NLT

The youngsters fell into line as their mama reprimanded them for their quarreling. Erin decided a good way to quell her kids' disputes was to have them march around the house quoting Scripture. After multiple occurrences, everyone felt the difference. The kids shared and played pleasantly. The Word of God did not return void but had implanted itself into their young hearts, yielding fruit.

When we commit to living a life led by the Spirit, we look differently at the world. We are grateful and we put others' needs ahead of our own. Our countenances shine a light on the goodness and love of the Savior within us. When we work to be at peace with others, no one can condemn us.

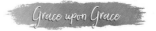

Grace upon Grace

Let others see Jesus in you by the way you represent him.

His Name

> "I made known to them your name, and I will continue to make it known that the love with which you have loved me may be in them, and I in them."

JOHN 17:26 ESV

Everyone was surprised when Ruth took the podium. No one expected the young widow to give the eulogy. She was calm as she shared precious memories. You could hear a pin drop until she called her two young children up by her side, and the crowd emotionally gasped. She proceeded to share what a great daddy he was and how he loved them all so much. His spirit would remain alive in them, and Ruth would see her beloved husband's face in theirs for the remainder of her days.

Jesus devotedly shared the Father with the disciples and his followers when he walked this earth. He desired that they know his name, character, and great love. The Savior continues this ministry from heaven enlightening us, as the Holy Spirit gives us insight through Scripture.

Grace upon Grace

Think of how you can make the Father's great love known.

The Pride Inside

What is the source of wars and fights among you? Don't they come from your passions that wage war within you?

JAMES 4:1 CSB

Ruthy felt irritated as her Bible study group discussed their interpretations of the Scripture passage. She wondered how they could have those opinions. She burst out, giving her viewpoint in a rather aggressive manner which was met with consternation. The next day during her quiet time, she realized it wasn't the others that made her so angry, it was the pride inside of her. Her desire to be seen as right in their eyes had caused her reaction.

Our egos aren't such subtle creatures. If you feel your blood pressure rising over a difference of opinion regarding spiritual things, take a moment. Step back and ask yourself if it is your pridefulness that is driving your feelings. Are your motives pure, evoking others to edifying God, or is there a divisive conversation going on? Have the same mindset as Jesus and be humble.

Grace upon Grace

Seek God's guidance before you speak and use your words to encourage others.

Trust in Christ

I have been crucified with Christ. It is no longer I who live, but Christ who lives in me. And the life I now live in the flesh I live by faith in the Son of God, who loved me and gave himself for me.

GALATIANS 2:20 ESV

A call came late one night that a heart had been found. The organ was being airlifted to the hospital and Emily must be prepped for surgery. She asked about her donor. It was a young man in good health but who died in a tragic car accident. His heart would live on it continued to beat inside Emily's chest. He had decided long ago to become a donor so he could give life to someone else if his life came to an end.

The greatest love was exhibited on the cross when Jesus died in our place and made us new. When we trust in Christ, our previous life expires, for he comes to live in us. The faith of a mustard seed is all he asks. We can be assured that when being crucified with him, we are indwelled with the divine miracle of his Holy Spirit. As we live for him, the world can see him in us. Have confidence in him, that his presence will shine through you illuminating his grace and love to everyone.

Grace upon Grace

Live like Jesus so that the people that you encounter see Christ.

Steadfast Love

Know therefore that the LORD your God, He is God, the
faithful God, who keeps His covenant and His faithfulness
to a thousand generations for those who love Him
and keep His commandments.

DEUTERONOMY 7:9 NASB

Joseph's word was golden. If he said he would do something,
you could count on it. There were no second thoughts and
no excuses even if a promise infringed on his personal plans.
People in the community who knew him admired him for
his kindhearted dependability. They knew if they tried to
bestow any honor on Joseph, he would resist it. When the
day came that he needed help, the whole town showed up.
They'd grown to care deeply for the trustworthy man.

What an incredible truth that the Creator is faithful to
those who love and obey him for a thousand generations.
Think of what a legacy is left to future family members
whose ancestors followed God's commands. We can affect
those coming after us by leaving a lifelong example of a
loving, sacrificial commitment to Christ.

Grace upon Grace

Leave a rich spiritual legacy by living with grace.

His Ideal Timing

The LORD directs the steps of the godly.
He delights in every detail of their lives.

PSALM 37:23 NLT

Junie's associate had gotten the promotion that she had wanted so badly. She arrived home in a grumpy mood and told her husband she didn't want to talk. Junie's beloved puppy had waited all day for her return, but when he tried to snuggle with her, she pushed him away. He coiled up in the corner, but after a while he approached her again. He nudged her hand and looked at her with his puppy-dog eyes, hoping she would respond. Her heart was humbled because of how carelessly she had dismissed him earlier. Junie began to consider the importance of her beloved family over the disappointment of that day.

Life is hard and things often go in the opposite direction from what we had hoped for. If we're throwing ourselves a pity party over not getting the recognition or opportunities we want, we should instead entrust ourselves to God. He controls the future, and if we will humble ourselves believing in his good plan, he will place us perfectly within his will and in his ideal timing.

Grace upon Grace

Try not to rush ahead to fulfill your wants or desires.

Life of Peace

The fruit of righteousness is sown in peace
by those who make peace.

JAMES 3:18 NKJV

It was not a matter of trying to win an argument but of never beginning it. Having struggled in the past with anger management, Aspen decided to get out of the way and let God fight her battles. Faithfully, she prayed for the ability to have self-control over her reactions and emotions. It was impossible for Aspen to accomplish this on her own but with her Savior in the driver's seat, she had faith that a life of peace was possible.

When we respond to someone in anger instead of speaking the truth in love, we exacerbate the situation. To desire the effects of a righteous life, we must give goodwill a priority position in all our dealings with others. Seek maturity in Christ by living a life that carries a commitment to restraint, wisdom, and peace.

Grace upon Grace

Spread love and peace so others will see Jesus in you.

Unbreakable Affection

"The mountains may move and the hills disappear,
but even then, my faithful love for you will remain.
My covenant of blessing will never be broken,"
says the LORD, who has mercy on you.

ISAIAH 54:10 NLT

"I love you here to there and back again!" said Deanna
to her curly-headed little girl. Bree would gleefully reply,
"Ditto!" It was their private saying, reserved only for each
other. Deanna would go on to explain that even though
hers was a forever love, there was someone who loved
Bree even more. His name was Jesus, and no matter what
happens or where her daughter may go, he would be with
her. "Has he been with you, too, Mommy?" asked the child.
"Every single second of my life," she replied.

What peace-filled truth that regardless of what befalls us,
God will be with us. His affection for us is unquenchable
and unconditional. We have the capacity through his Spirit
to live holy and righteous lives, being adopted into his
family by faith in Jesus. As his child, his blessings for us will
never cease. His mercy will always abound, and steadfast
love will abide with us forever.

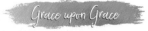

Grace upon Grace

Be amazed that God is always with you, loving and blessing
you through his grace and mercy.

Live in Humility

Arrogance leads to nothing but strife,
but wisdom is gained by those who take advice.

PROVERBS 13:10 CSB

Becca knew she was perfect for the office position, and no one else could match her qualifications. Although she had been told that they planned to promote from within the company, she sat in the outer office waiting for the boss to exit his office so she could follow him, declaring her superior abilities. When this finally struck his last nerve, he turned to make his own proclamation. Becca knew nothing about the one he planned to hire: her education and experience far surpassed Becca's. "You would be wise to add some humility to your skill set."

When our faces are to the ground and we lay in the dust, we should begin our confessions. God hates our pride, so in his love he humbles us. If we have been found with a high opinion of ourselves, we must confess and believe that God forgives us. We can then start afresh, asking the Holy Spirit to alert us when we idolize ourselves.

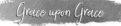

Grace upon Grace

Be quick to ask for forgiveness and seek to live in humility.

A Willing Servant

"Behold, I am the servant of the Lord;
let it be to me according to your word."
And the angel departed from her.

LUKE 1:38 ESV

Miriam was shocked to be considered worthy of joining
the ministry team. In fact, after receiving the call to pray
about accepting their invitation, her lack of self-worth
caused her to sit in stunned silence. She had petitioned God
about using her and had even told him that she would do
whatever he asked. Feeling unequipped for the new task,
she submitted herself to Jesus in faith that whatever he
called her to do, he could accomplish through her.

If you feel unprepared for the work God is calling you to
do, think about the men he chose as his disciples. They were
mostly uneducated fishermen. They were not chosen for
what they could bring to the cause. All they had was their
obedience and in Jesus' perspective. that was enough. God
is looking for those who will say yes, and he can use us just
as he used the disciples. All he needs is a willing servant.

Grace upon Grace

No matter how challenging, submit to God's will.

The Messiah

"Do not be afraid; for behold, I bring you good news of
great joy which will be for all the people; for today in the
city of David, there has been born for you a Savior,
who is Christ the Lord."

LUKE 2:10-11 NASB

The first Christmas Eve started as a normal night in the
field for the shepherds and their sheep. They had traveled
long and hard looking for the right pasture to feed and
bed down for the night. But that evening they would get
little sleep because a whole bunch of angels arrived to
announce the Messiah's birth in nearby Bethlehem. As
the heavenly host sang glory to God, the shepherd's fears
became wonder. They gathered their flocks and headed
into Bethlehem to see the Savior who would redeem all
mankind.

What joy surely accompanied the long-awaited promise
that the Messiah would come to deliver his people. The
Lord didn't announce the birth to high-profile kings but to
common shepherds. He wanted them to know that Jesus
was born for people like them. Regardless of where you've
been or what you've done, he came for you.

Grace upon Grace

Thank God for sending Jesus to save you:
a sinner who has become a child of God.

Almighty Conqueror

The LORD your God is with you,
the Mighty Warrior who saves.
He will take great delight in you;
in his love he will no longer rebuke you,
but will rejoice over you with singing.

ZEPHANIAH 3:17 NIV

On the night of the Savior's birth, the Father knew everything that would happen to Jesus in his earthly life. The road ahead would be fraught with rejection and the most vicious of deaths. But that first night in a stable, shepherds worshiped him, and his mother treasured every moment in her heart. God was well pleased with his Son. From baby, to teacher, to tortured substitute for our sins, Jesus is the risen Lord, and he did what he came to do—to save us.

Jesus' willingness to become man and to die in our place tore the curtain and gave us access to the Father. God and man now have an unrestricted relationship. Those who love him receive the assurance of his approval, the warmth of his joy, and the confidence that they're fully saved.

Grace upon Grace

Worship and adore Jesus, fully God and fully man,
Redeemer, and Lord.

Christlikeness

May the Lord direct your hearts into the love of God
and into the patience of Christ.

2 Thessalonians 3:5 nkjv

Rachel and Zoey worked diligently, cleaning and setting
up the room for the event. Meanwhile their co-worker was
on the phone gossiping with a friend. Deborah whispered
slanderous things between her sips of latte. She was
oblivious to the sweat dripping down the other women's
faces from their hard work. Zoey whispered complaints to
Rachel but in response, Rachel commented that they should
not hold a grudge for being left to carry the load. "Scripture
instructs us on how to appeal lovingly to an offense,"
she said. They both agreed to persevere and to confront
Deborah in the way God would do it.

The apostle Paul says to warn your brethren in Christ who
continue to be lazy and engage in idleness. Confrontations
are hard, but when they are done as Jesus would do them,
they can lead to righteousness.

Grace upon Grace

*Remember that you are accountable
for correcting others in love.*

Holy Justice

We know the one who said, "I will take revenge.
I will pay them back."
He also said, "The LORD will judge his own people."

HEBREWS 10:30 NLT

Three young college men stood before the court for sentencing. Although their crime was an immature misdemeanor, it wasn't the first offense for two of them. The third offender, Brent, had never broken the law before and had foolishly been drawn into the caper. Sylvain and Mario, however, were sentenced to a month in jail each, community service, and a hefty fine. Brent, being the novice culprit, received thirty days in jail with a lesser fine and a warning to change the company he kept.

None of us ever want to stand before an earthly judge, however, it is guaranteed that we will go before the heavenly justice. We, his children, will watch some of our earthly works burn. We serve a loving, compassionate Abba. He is a righteous, holy adjudicator. Rejoice in the knowledge that we, as Christ followers, have a Redeemer defending us.

Grace upon Grace

Praise him that your debt was paid in full on the cross.

Dying to Self

For me, to live is Christ and to die is gain.

PHILIPPIANS 1:21 CSB

Jada was as angry as a teen girl can get for having to spend her school break with her cousins in a podunk town. She felt like her life had been cancelled because she wouldn't get to be part of the plans with her city friends. Her parents thought spending time on the farm would give their privileged daughter a new perspective. So, Jada left behind her fun-filled break for what she anticipated to be weeks of boredom. When she got there, she adapted quickly to small community life. She learned that giving up what she wanted opened the door to something better.

For the Christian, dying to self and living for Jesus is the best life of all. We discover our purpose in knowing our Lord. Meaningfulness is added to our lives as we seek to help people. Loving like Jesus brings inexplicable joy.

Grace upon Grace

Die to self, so that you may gain life in Christ.

Keep Me Humble

The LORD sustains the humble
but casts the wicked to the ground.

PSALM 147:6 NIV

Michele dreaded the weekly contest to see who would move
up a few chairs in the high school choir. She usually sang so
softly the teacher would move on. She was happy staying in
the back row. This time the teacher decided to move around
the room. Michele prayed that she'd be passed over, but the
instructor stood right by her side. After hearing the beauty
of her voice, the choirmaster moved her to the first chair.
Michele decided to trust God because this unexpected
affirmation was actually an answer to prayer. She wanted to
sing professionally for Jesus.

When we put God first and trust his plan, we can be
comfortable in any position. If we're last, it's okay; if we're
in the spotlight, we can rest in his power to perform his will
through us. Placing ourselves in his care and being willing
to do whatever he wants without needing the accolades
is fertile ground for God to use. He knows whom he can
entrust with great things for his kingdom.

Grace upon Grace

Humbly lay your life on the altar for God's service.

Sacrifice Everything

They overcame him because of the blood of the Lamb and
because of the word of their testimony, and they did not
love their life even when faced with death.

REVELATION 12:11 NASB

The mission trip to Ethiopia would be spent living with the
village people and building trust so Christ's gospel could be
shared. Little did the missionaries know, two doors down
from their small abode lived a witch doctor. James and
Petra prayed for his salvation while he cast his incantations
for their demise. James shared the gospel with him while
Petra prayed for the conversation to be covered with the
blood of Jesus. It took more than once, but as the witch
doctor watched their testimony of love and service to the
community, the Spirit drew him in. The man received Christ
and the spiritual path of the whole village was changed.

We overcome the enemy when we stand firm in our faith
for Jesus. No matter what peril is in our path, when we die
to self and live for Christ, we're running the race well. When
we sacrifice everything for the cause of Christ, at life's finish
line we'll hear, "Well done, good and faithful servant."

Grace upon Grace

*Sacrifice your relationships, your job,
and your life to make Jesus known.*

Send Me

How can anyone preach unless they are sent?
As it is written: "How beautiful are the feet
of those who bring good news!"

ROMANS 10:15 NIV

It's the time of year when resolutions are made. There's a
sense of renewal, bright opportunities, and the hope of
open doors. This could be the year of a successful cure but
what good would it do if no one shares it? Knowing about
a cure without proclaiming it offers no value to anyone.
Having the answer to life, if it is not communicated,
delivers the worst of all deaths—an unnecessary one.

Scripture confronts us with the question of how the world
will be saved if we keep the truth to ourselves? How will
they know the extent of God's love? Where will they go
to hear if no one is speaking? How long will it take for
those who belong to Jesus before they go fulfill the Great
Commission? We must activate the beautiful feet who bring
the good news. We have the life-giving solution, the one
true salvation made available to all. May this be the year we
say, "Here I am Lord; send me."

Grace upon Grace

Say yes to Christ and live to share his salvation and grace.